CW01628359

The Art of the Maker

The Art of the Maker

Peter Dormer

THAMES AND HUDSON

For Jane Smith and Gertrude Dormer

Crafts Council Funded

British Library Cataloguing-in-Publication Data
A catalogue record for this book is available from the British Library.

ISBN 0-500-27778-8

Printed and bound in Spain

Contents

Acknowledgments

I wish particularly to thank Professor Christopher Frayling, Ann Hechle and Professor Neal French for their intelligent and good-humoured guidance and support. I am indebted to Jane Smith, Andrew Harrison, Professor John Onians, Sandy Heslop and Julia Hawkins for their advice. This essay was written with the aid of a grant from the Crafts Council, London. I owe particular thanks to Tony Ford, Barclay Price and Stephen Burroughs. I also thank the University of East Anglia Schools of World Art Studies and Music, and the Eastern Arts Board for awarding me a Fellowship in the Critical Appreciation of the Applied Arts which gave me time to finish the text. Any error and false argument that remains is my responsibility alone.

Peter Dormer
London 1994

Introduction

A hundred years ago the link between craft knowledge and the fine arts was taken for granted. Today the situation is different. In the fine arts some say that handicraft is dead.[1] In the applied arts there are those who argue that craft is separate from and very much secondary to the ideas that (it is said) are expressed by the objects.[2] The modern orthodoxy is that conception and execution are separate activities and that execution – mere making – can take care of itself. Skills are regarded as technical constraints upon self-expression and they are not recognized as being the content as well as the means of expression.

During the course of this essay I will discuss both applied and fine arts and because of this I have resurrected an old-fashioned phrase to cover them both: the plastic arts. By plastic arts I mean painting, sculpture and studio craft whose content is substantially dependent on practical skill, and whose intention is discovered through the process of making the object. Chapter One offers a description of craft knowledge, but throughout the book the terms skill, craft and tacit knowledge are all used to refer to knowledge that is learned practically through experience and that is demonstrated through practice. Craft is knowledge that must be demonstrated since it will not easily, if at all, be adequately conveyed through what can be said or written about it.

In the West a high value is placed on individuality and self-expression in the plastic arts. This emphasis on individuality has encouraged artists and studio craftspeople to search for unique forms, images and approaches to art. There is almost a degree of neurosis about being (and being seen to be) unique; about having something or being something inimitable. For example, Clement Greenberg, one of America's (and therefore the West's) most influential post-1945 art critics, wrote 'Conception (intuition/inspiration) alone belongs to individuals; everything else, including skill, can now be acquired by anyone'[3] and 'Inspiration is the only factor that cannot be copied'.[4]

Considering the postwar urgency for self-expression and individuality, it is possible to see why craft knowledge has become disdained. There is a view that craft knowledge, because it is communal (it has been created by many people), conflicts with originality. The prejudice against craft tends to be crude: craft, it is thought, is bound by rules, and it is assumed that rules necessarily conflict with freedom of thought, imagination and expression.

If the ultimate value in art is placed on uniqueness, and if craft knowledge is regarded as everyone's knowledge, then it is easy to argue that, in pursuit of uniqueness, craft knowledge can be dispensed with altogether. For a number of artists and studio craftspeople craft knowledge is a threat: according to the modern orthodoxy it applies a brake upon the creative imagination. It is assumed that absorbing craft knowledge necessarily forces your thinking through a filter of one set of rules. It is also assumed that if you are skilled then you are drawn irresistibly, as though beguiled by Sirens, into practising skill as an end in itself.

The following are among the prejudices about craft knowledge that I have identified:

a) Craft knowledge is merely mechanical.
b) Craft knowledge can be learned as and when you need it.
c) Craft knowledge and 'having ideas' or 'being creative' are separate activities.
d) Craft knowledge is separable from making aesthetic judgments.
e) Craft knowledge is rule-based and rules conflict with personal creativity.
f) Craft knowledge is about forming habits, and habits also conflict with or inhibit creativity.

My thesis is, first, that each of these prejudices is mistaken; secondly, that the plastic arts benefit from a 'traditional' approach, which recognizes that process and content are interdependent; thirdly, that craft knowledge itself enriches individual experience and becomes a part of the self that is expressed in art or studio craft.

Although conservationist in its argument, this essay is not intended to be reactionary. But just as we worry about the continuation of non-Western cultures threatened by the technology of the West, so too should we be concerned to safeguard and encourage parts of Western culture that are in danger of being lost.

I believe that practical skill – handicraft – is undervalued. It is out of fashion in the art world, it is misunderstood, it is neglected. My arguments are that we might easily lose a tradition of making and thinking-through-making in the plastic arts and that this loss would be a serious one.

My argument is not, however, an attack on other developments in the visual arts. It does not dismiss the many new forms of visual exploration that have been current, such as performance, installation and video art – it is simply that these are not the concern of this essay. My concern is with art in which handicraft (usually that of the artist or studio craftsperson) is the crucial, the only link between intention and expression.

1 What Is Craft Knowledge?

This chapter deals with the nature of craft and practical thinking. Although it is not restricted to the plastic arts these, naturally, are the focus.

Understanding how things work is one of life's pleasures and our greatest asset in the pursuit of this pleasure is language. Language is the principal means by which we analyse our probings in the world and reflect upon what we may have discovered or invented. Language gives us (or enhances) the power of conceptual thought and, as modern science demonstrates, reflecting theoretically on practical matters can be immensely useful. The physicist Joseph Schwartz demonstrates this in his book *The Creative Moment*[1] by considering the example of the development of the steam engine.

In the eighteenth and nineteenth centuries, engineers developed the steam engine into a more refined and efficient machine. These were practical men, and whether or not they were scientifically literate, they kept records and published reliable technical data. The engineers, their clients and theoreticians began to wonder if a steam engine could ever be 100 per cent efficient. Sadi Carnot, a French engineer and soldier, set to speculating about an ideal steam engine and concluded that the ideal was not attainable. The encapsulation of his findings by the German mathematical physicist Rudolf Clausius in the First and Second Laws of Thermodynamics has saved many people much fruitless work. These laws are an example of a mode of reasoning whose principles, no matter what your colour, gender, nationality or religious belief, hold, with or without your agreement.

This example is but one of a thousand illustrations that we might turn to as evidence of the useful interaction between practical and theoretical knowledge. However, it also alerts us to a distinction between the two kinds of knowledge. The Laws of Thermodynamics – theoretical knowledge – cannot tell you how to build a single engine.[2] To build an engine demands the practical knowledge of the engineer and the machinist – which is complex; much of it defies description in words. It is, as will be discussed, 'tacit' knowledge. Tacit knowledge or 'know-how' is immensely powerful: it gets things built. But it is also slowly acquired. If we had to rely on discovering ideas through craft, through plodding empiricism, then we might never have progressed as far as steam engines, let alone beyond them. The power of theoretical knowledge is that it provides general insights into how fields of action work and how we might improve our practice. Theoretical knowledge has been described as a springboard.[3]

In our everyday world, in which buildings are constructed, consumer goods manufactured, illnesses cured and art created, the concept alone is not enough. Physical effort must be made: often this requires practical expertise. Experimental scientists must understand their apparatus; technologists have to experiment to find ways of turning scientific discoveries into tools and products. And the rest of us are involved in these endeavours because we help to produce or sell or buy or use the things that are made.

The knowledge required to make something work is not the same as understanding the principle behind it. Practical knowledge appears to have the following characteristics:

a) Craft knowledge is not easily described by language, and in many cases resists a complete description. Writing about an action, talking about an action, and reflecting upon the nature of an action are not the same thing as the action itself, nor do they provide much insight into how it feels to act and how it feels to know for oneself how to act.
b) Craft knowledge is often difficult or even impossible to translate into theory or to encode (for the purposes of computing) into mathematical or logical languages.
c) Craft knowledge is not something you think about if you are expert in it: as an expert you do not think about the exercise of your craft. You do, however, think about extending your expertise and about the goals to which you are applying it.
d) Craft knowledge is harder to acquire through books than it is face to face with a skilled practitioner and teacher.

Craft knowledge is sometimes called local knowledge as distinct from generalizable knowledge. Generalizable knowledge gives us the Second Law of Thermodynamics which says, in essence, that for every 10 cents of energy you put into a machine you will be lucky to get 9 cents back (and never 10 cents). Local knowledge is your ability to make a machine that works at all.

Confirmation of the power and the peculiarity of local knowledge is everywhere, but it is so much a part of everyday experience that it is taken for granted. Anecdotal evidence for its presence is abundant. Michael Polanyi, physicist, sociologist and philosopher, whose work in the field of practical knowledge is discussed below, described how the indefinable knowledge that people have, which nevertheless resists written, verbal or even mathematical description, can confound technology: 'I have myself watched in Hungary a new, imported machine for blowing lamp bulbs, the exact counterpart of which was operating successfully in Germany, failing for a whole year to produce a single flawless bulb.'[4]

I recently interviewed a product engineer working on the manufacture of car crash test dummies who describes something similar. His small design and engineering company was working with several European firms on the development of a new, sophisticated dummy for testing the impact of collisions in cars. The dummy is designed to react like a live human being and to give consistent test results crash after crash. This European consortium and a North American competitor are both obliged by law to make the drawings of their patents public but, the engineer explained, it does not offer a competitive advantage. 'We cannot make their dummy come right from their drawings, they cannot make our dummy come right from ours.' The important knowledge is lodged locally – in the minds and hands of their respective workforces.[5]

A well-researched catalogue of the phenomenon of local knowledge is provided by Professor Harry Collins, a sociologist of science, in his book *Changing Order* (1985). Collins describes in one example what happened when rival groups of scientists tried to build a laser machine in the early 1980s. The type of laser, called a TEA (Transversely Excited Atmospheric pressure CO_2), was then new but the groups had visited a working example in Canada. There was intense competition to replicate it.

As he followed the groups trying to replicate a TEA laser, Collins saw that although the scientists understood the theory and had the components in the right places, they could not puzzle out why the laser failed to work.[6]

A group led by a scientist called Harrison, for instance, tried to solve the problem by changing the thickness and the length of the wiring; they also cleaned the glass tube with extra care. After five months of puzzles a solution began to emerge: 'Finally, short of anything else to do, at about 5.15pm, Harrison completely removed the connecting wire from the spark gap and tried again. Suddenly an arc discharge took place between the plates; a great cheer greeted it.'[7] It was a hunch that paid off.

Despite seeming to be a good copy of one that was already functioning elsewhere, it had taken Harrison many months to get his own laser to work. Interestingly, he made a second laser that worked in just two days.

Neither the theory, nor his observations of the working laser he was trying to replicate, gave Harrison the knowledge he required to make one of his own. He was without the local knowledge. Moreover, although he had asked questions of the pioneering team that had built the original, successful machine they had only answered what he had asked: they did not volunteer information for questions that he could not see were relevant.

Collins draws a number of conclusions from his studies, including: a) that transfer of skill-like knowledge is capricious and b) that skill-like knowledge travels best (or only) through accomplished practitioners. If the scientists who had created the original machine had volunteered information then Harrison would not have been frustrated for five months.

There is a moral as well as an epistemological dimension to debates about practical knowledge. An Austrian philosopher, Allan Janik, has identified a problem with Western philosophy, starting with Socrates: that it has failed to take working life seriously.[8] He excludes Karl Marx, Ludwig Wittgenstein and Leo Tolstoi from this failure – all of whom believed that humanly useful practical work was an integral part of any life that was worth living.

The search for a 'fulfilling life' through practical activity has become a major concern in the West this century. For example, the search is at the heart of the sprawling arts and crafts movement where men and women have built their lives around commercially obsolete technologies such as hand dyeing and weaving, pottery, furniture making, glass blowing and the like. The 'fulfilment' appears to be dependent upon their having turned their craft into an art. This is discussed in Chapter Five, pp. 72-7.

Interest in the nature of practical work has roots in ergonomics. The way in which people think, make practical inferences, receive information and solve unpredicted practical crises is of vital interest to designers of complex systems such as nuclear power stations, air traffic control centres and other operations where there is a continuous co-operation between teams of people and complex technology. Here, if such interactions go wrong then the consequences of a mistake could kill them – and us. Again the epistemology of practical work is closely shadowed by moral considerations.

In recent years a number of international conferences have been held about practical knowledge. One of the most influential was 'Culture, Language and Artificial Intelligence'[9] held in Stockholm in 1988, where speakers explored the concept of tacit knowledge. Tacit knowledge is the preferred phrase for craft knowledge among academics. Both senses of the word 'tacit' are relevant: a) implied without direct expression, understood; b) silent.

Tacit knowledge refers to a body of knowledge which we have gained through experience – both through the experience of our senses and through the experience of doing work of various kinds. Tacit knowledge differs from propositional knowledge in that it cannot easily be articulated or described in words. Nor can tacit knowledge be described mathematically. This inability to describe the core of a craft becomes more and more acute the closer the craft comes to being an 'art'. The particular 'touch' of a violinist, pianist, draughtsman, surgeon, nurse or vet cannot be described, but it can be demonstrated and, to a degree, be imitated or even learned wholly by someone else.[10]

It is also argued that propositional knowledge, although normally held in higher regard than tacit or practical knowledge, is underpinned by practical knowledge. Professor David Pye, designer, writer and craftsperson, has argued before that the designer is in the hands of the craftsperson.[11] If the craftsperson cannot 'do', then the designer cannot specify. Often designers do not or cannot specify (because it is impracticable) what needs to be done. They may specify a goal instead. The designer, for instance, wants a tabletop in wood. She or he specifies the timber and the dimensions of the tabletop, as well as the shape and any details (niches, chamfers), but not how they are to be achieved. The craftsperson must be able to imagine what the result should look like. The designer relies on the craftsperson's imagination and skill in interpreting the designer's wish, as well as the technical know-how.

Practical activity such as designing is not always underpinned by the practical arts. The aeronautical engineer, Barnes Wallis, described how he 'drew' the shape for the successful airship the R100 (not to be confused with the disastrous R101). He did not draw it, he arrived at the shape in his head through a mathematical equation.[12]

Nevertheless, much of the time the Pye thesis holds good – we are in the hands of the practitioners and the doers. But there is another caveat: if we have to rely on other people's tacit knowledge, then we want some assurance that their knowledge is real. There is a great deal of mythology associated with craft – and with professional practice generally.

There is often a temptation when considering craft knowledge to drop the guard of scepticism and to treat with laxity such vague and often opportunistic claims about 'intuition'; for a tension exists between the objectivity of science and the subjectivity of tacit knowledge. The myth prevails of the 'dumb artisan' (tacit, taciturn) who, because he or she cannot explain what is being done, appears to proceed unintelligently with a mixture of received traditions and intuitions. Science appears to set a standard of clarity and precision which a non-scientific approach cannot match.

When discussing tacit knowledge it is easy to make unsubstantiated claims. If knowledge is to be useful (for it to count as knowledge) there must be ways of subjecting it to public scrutiny. Craft knowledge may be hard to define but it is not ineffable.

In his play *Murmuring Judges*, David Hare demonstrates the dangers of tacit knowledge.[13] One of the central characters, Sir Peter Edgecombe, is a leading lawyer, who speaks to a junior employee about the craft of being a lawyer:

> After a while you do develop an instinct. That's one of the things a first-rate advocate has. Your profession, after all, is the judgment of people. After a while, you have certain skills. It's not even conscious. It becomes animal. It's a gut instinct. Here. [*He points to his heart.*] I'd say, if anything, it's the crucial ability. You're asked to walk every day through a minefield of lies. If nothing else, you do develop a certain forensic capacity for knowing when someone is telling the truth.

Hare goes on to use this speech to destroy the audience's confidence in Sir Peter's character. Irina, the employee to whom he is talking, has allowed Sir Peter to take her occasionally to the opera and to dinner and has (tacitly) let him believe she liked him rather than going out with him because he was her employer. Irina puts Sir Peter's tacit skills to the test:

IRINA: When we had dinner ... I said how much I'd enjoyed it.
[*Sir Peter smiles*]

SIR PETER: You did.

IRINA: What a wonderful evening I'd had. [*She pauses, dangerous.*]
Now, please, I'd be interested, answer me forensically, what's your opinion? You say you know about these things.
Was I telling the truth?

The audience knows Irina had dined with Sir Peter for expediency rather than pleasure. The play develops with Sir Peter refusing to recognize that what he 'knows' may only have the status of prejudice.

What startled me about Hare's fictional Sir Peter and his argument from tacit knowledge was how easily it could have been cited as real evidence for the nature of tacit knowledge at a conference on skill. I imagined a researcher interviewing lawyers and getting excited as each one confirmed that practical experience could give an intuitive feel for the truth.

For comparison, I quote here the non-fictional text of a nurse's commentary in a paper at the Stockholm Conference:

> I cannot formulate the deeper dimension of my knowledge. I cannot describe how I tell a patient that he is going to die. I have built up the most important part of my knowledge by meeting people and learning. This is what is crucial to my ability to make a diagnosis. It is a question of doing it again and again. This is always impossible to express in words. After many years' experience as a nurse many of my reflections are mechanical. I see what is going to happen and without formulating it myself ... I would like to inculcate in young nurses the view that every patient is a new experience. This cannot be learned theoretically; more than anything else it requires an ability to 'see'.[14]

The nurse differs from the fictional Sir Peter in that she looks at each patient as a 'new experience'. She rejects the prejudice of 'I know this type, I've seen it all before'.

But on the other hand the comparison is still telling. Those of us who are keen to raise the status of practical and tacit knowledge are perhaps over-inclined to indulge an assertion of intuition from someone such as a nurse, especially if this assertion is backed by years of experience of caring. Such indulgence may be misplaced. We do not accept the word of a lawyer or a policeman who argues 'I know I'm right'. To call on tacit knowledge is not enough for a conviction – we rightly want proof.

Fortunately, most craft activity is open to assessment and criticism. The most important component of the craftsperson's work is what he or she does: we have as the centre of our scrutiny the object or the activity itself, whether a table or a performance of a violin concerto.

Some forms of specialized craft knowledge such as those which, it is claimed, turn the craft to an art, are especially troubling to the sceptic. Michael Polanyi writes of what he calls the need for 'destructive analysis' to be applied to claims of tacit knowledge.[15] He demonstrates this approach by applying it to a subject debated in the world of piano-playing – the claim that some pianists bring a kind of special 'touch' to their work which distinguishes and elevates it above that of other pianists.

Polanyi explains that when a key is depressed, a hammer is set in motion which hits a string. The hammer is pushed by the depressed key, is flung into free motion for a short distance and is eventually stopped by the string. The effect of the hammer on the string is determined by the speed of the hammer in free motion at the moment when it hits the string; it should make no difference how the hammer acquired the speed. In other words, it should not make any difference whether it was an amateur or a virtuoso who hit the key. This analysis, based on empirical observation, so far destroys the claim that there is anything special about the way a pianist 'touches' the keys. Further research, however, revealed information that validates the claims in favour of 'touch', confirming that the way the keys are pressed does indeed have an effect on the sound. The keys themselves make a sound each time they are depressed. This was discovered by removing the strings and striking the keys. 'This noise can be varied while the speed imparted to the hammer remains unaltered. The noise mingles with the note sounded by the hammer on the string and modifies its quality, and this seems to account in principle for the pianist's capacity to control the tone of the piano by the art of his or her touch.'[16]

Tacit knowledge may be impossible to articulate precisely, but it may certainly be demonstrated: the virtuoso knows how in a way the amateur does not.

Craft knowledge is generally disciplined knowledge, as disciplined as applied science. Craft knowledge also makes use of a concrete, precise verbal and written language. This language does not adequately describe the actual carrying out of a process because in any description of a practical activity too much that is important gets left out. Nonetheless, every craft has a technical language.

Consider this description by the novelist and aeronautical engineer Nevil Shute of a craftsperson working at a lathe. It comes from his novel *Trustee from the Toolroom*.[17] The hero is a toolmaker called Keith Stewart who is described here making a present for his niece, some metal eggs to go with her toy duck:

> He picked a three-inch end of inch-diameter steel rod out of the scrap box, put it in the three-jaw chuck, started the lathe, and chamfered the

> end to forty-five degrees. A lifetime of such work had made him very quick; in a minute he was working with a hand-scraper on a rest, turning the end of the steel to form the large end of the egg, talking to the little girl all the time. Three emery sticks of successive fineness followed the scraper, and the large end was finished. He brought forward the parting tool and parted off the piece one-and-a-half inches long down to a diameter of about a quarter of an inch, and chamfered the small end shape roughly by the careful manipulation of a knife tool in the four tool post. Then came careful work again with the hand-scraper, then the final parting off. He gave the warm, nearly finished egg to the little girl to hold while he found a one-inch bore copper collar and put it in the chuck. Then he put the egg in it, small end outwards, and pinched it up, using the tailstock centre to set it roughly true, started the lathe again, and went to work very gently with the hand-scraper and the emery sticks till he had it finished to his satisfaction. Then he took it from the lathe, gave it a final burnish on a rouge polishing mop at the tool grinder …

The scene goes on to describe how, by heating it, he gives the shiny egg some colour. 'Then he gave it to Janice, a deep, brilliantly blue egg.'

Craft knowledge frequently uses precise language whose beauty derives from the craftsperson's close knowledge of the material, the tools and the processes. Such language can indicate the real components of a craft's discipline. We test the language against the practice. If a metalworker says he can do this or that we ask him to demonstrate. Meanwhile, other knowledgeable people, metalworkers themselves, perhaps, would judge whether or not the work was 'good enough'. This judgment would derive from a consensus among practitioners based not only on their experience, but on existing objects which display excellence in that craft.

Public scrutiny is a key element in the development of tacit knowledge. It is not enough for a craftworker to say 'I know how to do this'. The knowledge has to be demonstrated and it will be assessed by peers against what is held to be good current practice. What counts as good practice will often rely on the question 'Is it working?'

However, craft knowledge is two-headed: it has a public aspect, which includes 'destructive analysis' and the judgment of other practitioners, and a private aspect: craft knowledge resides in individual people. Such knowledge becomes a part of the self. There are no means of describing that knowledge adequately – even to oneself.

In most complex crafts there is, for those expert in it, a form of dialogue going on between the practitioner, his expertise, and the goal that the practitioner is trying to make or find. Dialogue is not quite the right word, partly because in order to make progress an expert must know rely on his or her expertise without concern.

Consider the following quotation from *A Stepladder to Painting* by Jan Gordon, a British painter active in the mid-twentieth century, who was especially regarded as a thoughtful teacher. It is a painter's manual of the kind that is out of fashion but a part of my thesis is that the knowledge which good manuals contain should be re-evaluated rather than disparaged.

Gordon's book is a careful guide to the knowledge of painting that any painter ought to want to acquire. He describes the knowledge that a painter will acquire through the proper study of still-life painting. The book as a whole treats the complexities of representational painting, although much is of benefit to any painter:

> A full two-thirds of the real job of art is mental, and the more you know what you are after the more you will be able to make your subconscious (action) and conscious (structure) intentions work in double harness ... As long as you fumble at your job the subconscious is in bondage and can only operate by lucky spasms.[18]

Gordon presents the notion of a painter searching for a painterly goal through the creation of a picture – a portrait, say, or a still-life. This goal might be the expression of an atmosphere, emotion or characteristic that the artist perceives in the subject and wishes to reveal through the painting. The search for both the goal and the means is a mental activity – it will include consideration of colour analysis, measurement, and other particulars that the artist thinks will be germane to the finding and capturing of the goal.

For example, suppose as a painter you wish to capture and convey the quality of an empty urban street at noon on a hot summer's day.

In order both to explore and accomplish the goal you need to be able to rely on your knowledge of colour, tone, devices of illusion including one-, two-, three-point and colour perspective, and also to know how your materials will behave. The more craft knowledge you have the more you can tackle pictorial problems that emerge as you move towards your goal.

Craft knowledge not only enables you to achieve your goal, it also enables you to imagine what your goal might look like. It becomes not merely the means of achieving the goal but the means of visualizing it in the first place. Craft expertise (more than mere competence) allows the subject to be explored in full confidence of the expert's ability to find solutions. For example, suppose one of the desired effects is to convey the kind of heat that makes everyone feel and everything look torpid. You perhaps discern that mixing a little crimson into some burnt umber and setting it against another colour achieved with ultramarine and azure blue might assist the effect. Perhaps lightly scumbling one colour against a denser layering of the other colour will enhance the effect.

The mental goal – torpid heat – is dependent on the knowledge of the craft that will effect that goal. And then, reflecting on what you have done, you may decide whether it works or not; if not, then the problem must be identified and worked through again. The action and the intention work in harness. We know we want to put a modified burnt umber against a modified azure blue but we do not have to think about the precise tone or the hue – we just do it. If it looks wrong, we simply rectify it.

Without the ability to act expertly we could not progress. Indeed, we could not accomplish our goals without the great difficulty. It is evident from the quotation from Nevil Shute that the craftsman acts quickly, fluently and with certainty – none of which would be possible if he was thinking about how he should do the task.

Craft knowledge, although we will have acquired much of it consciously and laboriously, achieves the status of a skill once it is taken for granted and not considered in pursuit of our goals.

In *Personal Knowledge*, Michael Polanyi begins a section on skills with a maxim: 'The aim of a skilful performance is achieved by the observance of a set of rules which are not known as such to the person following them.'[19] There are (at least) two different ways in which these rules can be unknown. They might always be unknown, or they become 'unknown'. Riding a bicycle is an example of the first. Millions of people can ride a bike, yet no one knows how they ride a bike, nor can they tell anyone else how to ride a bike, although plenty of people can tell a cyclist how to improve after conquering the essentials of moving forward, maintaining a balance, and avoiding obstacles. One does not learn to ride a bike by looking at the rules.

The second point, as Jan Gordon makes clear, is that rules are learnt and then, as one becomes expert, 'forgotten' (they become second nature and we take them for granted). However, the nature of rules and skill is not plain and further refinement of the notion of rules occurs throughout this essay and in particular in Chapter Four, pp. 61-70.

Not all knowledge that is not put into words is tacit knowledge. As Allan Janik explains, there are various categories of knowledge that may be called tacit but that can be expressed in words if desired. For example, it suits craft guilds and a number of professional bodies to add 'value' to their services by creating a mystique about what they do. Keeping knowledge secret is best done if it is not written down but passed on from person to person, with each one sworn to secrecy. This is closed-shop protectionism, not tacit knowledge.

Tacit knowledge in its proper sense, in the sense used in this essay, is explained by Janik as referring 'to those aspects of experience which are wholly knowable self-reflectively ... but by their very nature are incapable of precise articulation.'[20]

An example of this is provided by the British painter Patrick Heron, an eloquent writer who is both an expert on and admirer of the painter Henri Matisse. Here is Heron's eloquent attempt at describing Matisse's painting *Deux Fillettes, Fond Rouge et Verte* (1947): 'The aesthetic experiences, the spatial sensations, are utterly concrete: they bowl us over, they are totally present to one's visual senses, yet to explain them seems increasingly impossible. At best one can hope, very inadequately, to describe them.'[21]

Janik takes his concept of practical knowledge and divides it into two broad areas: the knowledge of familiarity and the knowledge acquired through doing and making.[22]

The knowledge of familiarity is grounded in experiencing sensations; it is knowledge that is gained through the senses. A simple example, much loved by professional philosophers, is the smell of coffee. The only way one gets to know what coffee smells like is to smell it. No amount of description can give someone an understanding of what it is to experience the smell of roast coffee.

A great deal of that knowledge called connoisseurship is knowledge of the senses – and it is exceedingly valuable – not only in the connoisseurship of tasting foods and wine, or in the connoisseurship of art attribution, but in the connoisseurship of diagnosing problems. It is surprising, for instance, how much diagnosis depends upon connoisseurship – a mechanic or engineer has as much need to acquire the familiarity of problems through his or her senses as a doctor. The way an engine sounds or the way a mechanism responds to the touch are revealing to the knowledgeable engineer. And a doctor or a nurse is often a connoisseur of tactile and auditory, as well as visual, signs in a patient. The nuances of breathing, the weight and tension of a muscle, the feel of the skin or even the smell of a patient are important aspects of connoisseurship or, as it is otherwise termed, the knowledge of familiarity.

People who study art or deal in it talk colloquially of 'getting their eye in'. Art connoisseurship tends to be concerned either with the correct attribution of works of art to individual artists or with public assertions as to the aesthetic merits of a given work of art.

In attribution the concern is to state whether a picture is by 'x', a copy of 'x', by a follower of 'x', in the manner of 'x' or from the 'school of x'. It is far from being an exact 'science' but museums, auction houses, collectors and dealers depend upon it. In recent years advances in scientific analysis as well as scholarship has reduced but not supplanted the role of the educated eye in the attribution of works of art.

The situation regarding connoisseurship in the plastic arts becomes different when the task is not the attribution of a work of art to a named artist or school of art but the judging of whether or not a piece of art has merit. This difficult task is done not only by art critics writing about art exhibitions for the newspapers and the art press but throughout art colleges in Europe and North America where tutors and examiners award marks to individual works of art and grade them for examination.

Debates about 'merit' only make sense within an agreed system of values. Some commentators wonder if talking or writing about artistic merit in the context of Western contemporary plastic art at this stage of the twentieth century is now a meaningless exercise. There is no agreed framework of values and consequently there can be no real connoisseurship; there are just private opinions publicly expressed and jostling for attention. This issue is discussed in Chapter Six.

Connoisseurship is not to be confused with mere whim or even opinion. Connoisseurship in more rigorous disciplines, such as classical music, medicine or car mechanics, is real, substantial knowledge because it relates to a number of empirical possibilities that can be tested.

The knowledge of familiarity is acquired through constant exposure to the subject and a gradual tutoring of one's senses. One's ability to see patterns, discriminate between similar but different qualities and to recognize nuances is an extended dialogue of testing with the subject over a long period of time. It is done within a framework of values and usually it is accomplished by talking to other people and conferring with their judgments.

The other category of tacit knowledge identified by Janik – that of 'know-how' – involves the learning of specific pieces of information and techniques. One of his examples comes from cooking. Janik says that although cooking may seem 'banal to minds fascinated by the arcana of computer programming' it is epistemologically interesting. With regard to cooking you will not be able to follow even the clearest recipes without first having mastered simple but specific techniques. 'For example, the distinction, so fundamental to cooking, between beating and folding is almost impossible to formulate in writing ... on the other hand it is absolutely simple to master if someone shows you the difference.'[23]

Take the example of learning the piano. One has to be drilled to eliminate mistakes: here one can talk of a right and a wrong way to play. Once the technique is mastered, the rules of right and wrong playing that guided one through the novice stage are forgotten. When one is able to play a piano sonata, the rules may be extended. Janik says that learning may well involve drilling and rote-learning, but that once the rules are mastered, one has the freedom to be creative with them.[24]

This is the message argued by people such as Gordon: that practical expertise is open-ended. Yet, as the next chapter discusses, this message is both unfashionable and irrelevant to a substantial number of practitioners of the plastic arts and studio crafts.

In a general sense tacit knowledge is an aspect of all thinking, including conceptual thinking in such disciplines as mathematics, theoretical physics or philosophy. There is a craft to such thinking and one learns it, becomes expert, and applies it to solve problems. Moreover, it is possible that a philosopher or a physicist or a mathematician may say that he or she knows more, in the sense of understanding, than he or she can practically describe – whether in words or mathematical or logical notation.

But I want to claim for practical work a special sense of tacit knowledge, which is that the core of practical craft, in bodies of knowledge as various as oil painting and lace making, is in principle unrecoverable by words, that its presence can only be demonstrated, not described. Whereas, with tacit knowledge in the conceptual arts I argue that complete descriptions of the core of such knowledge are, in principle, recoverable by language because language is the medium in which the craft of conceptual thinking resides. The thinking in the crafts of oil painting, pottery, modelling, lace making and so forth resides not in language, but in the physical processes involving the physical handling of the medium.

2 Craft Skills and the Plastic Arts

Within the plastic arts, the status of craft knowledge or tacit knowledge has declined sharply because it is held to have no intrinsic value. This is not a new development of the last thirty years but it is, I believe, an accelerating decline. It is also considered that craft can be learned easily enough if required.[1] Consequently no great premium has been placed upon preserving or conserving systems for teaching craft knowledge.

A number of factors have encouraged the flight from tacit knowledge: the development of reductionist abstract art, the widespread use of installation, performance and other non-traditional, non-craft-based media, and the substitution of craft knowledge with art theory as the unifying body of knowledge taught as fine arts in Western art schools.

Since the Second World War artists have explored Abstract Expressionism, Color-field painting, Minimalism and Conceptualism. These movements secured a dominance that reduced the creation of traditionally crafted objects – such as realistic painting or sculpture – to a marginal activity. The marginality of craft was further increased by the expansion of fine arts into performance, installation and video art. These art forms are understandable responses to the nature of consumer, media-orientated society. Moreover, they may demand an exacting craft to make them work.

The intellectual intention behind installation and video arts is often sound. There is a sense in which traditional art forms, such as sculpture or painting, are too static, too slow or too mute to appeal to artists living in a world where a commonplace television commercial can convey a complete mini-drama in forty-five seconds. Consequently, to make a political, cultural, moral or sceptical comment, as many artists wish to, then assemblage, installation, video and similar 'quick' forms of art are obviously suitable strategies. The artist can take the techniques of electronic media and turn them into a mirror to reflect and comment upon the mores and prejudices of contemporary culture and society.

The attraction of installation, video and performance to contemporary artists, most of whom have little handicraft training, is that a video or an installation can be made without specialist knowledge. And videos and installations share with performance art the merits of being direct media – you can start making art straight away because you, the individual, write your own rules of construction, or choreography, or what you do with the video camera (designed as an idiot-proof, 'point and shoot' tool for the mass consumer market). Ironically, it is arguable that installation, performance and video art have become like run of the mill, nineteenth-century European narrative painting – mechanical procedures with a tendency towards the expression of vague moral sentiments.

The plastic arts have moved away from handicraft because craft knowledge is difficult to learn and too slow to acquire for the contemporary student or artist who wants to establish a personal style quickly in order to respond to a fast-changing art world.

An emphasis upon individuality in art has also aided the decline of craft. The acquisition of craft knowledge entails learning rules and imitating other people's work. Both these aspects are discussed in Chapters Three, pp. 45-6, pp. 50-5, and Four, pp. 61-9. To learn a craft entails, for a while at least, working in the fashion of one's teachers and mentors. In reality this is not, or need not be, a hindrance to individual creativity. But the assumption that craft knowledge is 'other people's rules' and that these are an infringement of self-expression is strong.

The professional art world is full of contradictions. It appears diverse in its activity and tolerant of many different sorts of art. The contemporary art world also appears to suggest that by saying 'I am an artist' and 'This is art if I say so', then you are an artist. The reality is different.

Success in the art world depends on an understanding of the orthodoxies of the moment and knowing how far these orthodoxies can manipulated, broken or ignored.

An orthodoxy of modernism, which is still strong, is that craft knowledge is separable from meaning in the visual arts – that technique is merely the means by which ideas are executed rather than conceived. An appeal to the intrinsic virtues of craft knowledge in art is currently regarded as either professionally quixotic or philistine.

Few artists become wealthy, but many hope to achieve the respect and recognition of their peers. Consequently, most ambitious professional artists, like ambitious professionals in any discipline, are emotionally unwilling to differ from the dominant ideology of their chosen profession. They experience two contradictory emotions and demands: one is a desire to be original, the other is to produce 'meaningful' art – one might say 'meaningful to the art world'.

It might be the case that 'Art is whatever you say is art', but the reality is that this statement is only significant if other artists agree to recognize the artist and the art as such. Any outsider can call what they make 'art' but it will not carry any weight unless the 'profession' agrees. The profession includes art curators, art critics, art theorists and the editors of art magazines. To be a successful artist is to understand the tacit prejudices and the orthodoxies of the day.

Craft, for example, is not recognized as art (irrespective of any English dictionary definition). The efforts of studio craftspeople to get themselves accepted as artists are often wasted. Acceptance now depends on denying or subverting craft, or insisting that craft is the least important aspect of the work. Even then, a work in what is perceived to be a craft medium, such as clay or glass or textiles, is seldom accepted as art. Such orthodoxies and prejudices may be unfair or illogical, but they exist; they are as common as the prejudices of social distinction, manners and class which permeate North American and European society.

The power of the dominant peer group in any profession is immense – and it is no less so in art. There is a poignant story, provided by the American academic Rosalind Krauss, which, even if it has become 'mythologized' over the years, does at least serve as a description of the professional artist's situation. Krauss was in a gallery with the critic Michael Fried. They were looking at a painting by Frank Stella from the period when he was painting flat, non-representational, non-illusionistic striped paintings.

A student entered and, pointing to the painting, asked Fried: 'What's so good about that?'

Fried replied, 'Look, Stella spends hours studying Velazquez ...What he would like more than anything else is to paint like Velazquez. But what he knows is that this is an option that is not open to him. So he paints stripes.'[2]

So-called 'flat' paintings were all that the dominant ideology at the time, inspired by critic Clement Greenberg, 'permitted'.

There are two other contemporary groups of people with influence on the careers of artists apart from artists themselves: art theorists and curators of art, both of whom take a negligible interest in the relationship between craft and art.

Theory was a crucial ingredient of minimalist and conceptual art during the mid-1960s. These two movements are perhaps more significant in the history of the decline of craft knowledge than Abstract Expressionism, Color-field painting and Pop Art. Minimalism and Conceptualism were rooted in philosophy and therefore dispensed with tacit knowledge almost entirely. The physical objects were aesthetically simple and relatively unimportant, the real objects being the theories they 'represented'.

Minimalist and conceptualist art are not identical movements. To some extent Minimalism depends on there being an object. But Conceptualism bade farewell to the object. The British critic John A. Walker has explained that one of the goals of conceptual art was the 'dematerialization of the art object'. So certain artists, such as Victor Burgin,[3] wrote down instructions which can be photocopied. To follow these instructions is to experience a conceptual work by Burgin. This way, Walker says, art becomes free from museums, art galleries and commerce.[4] It also becomes free of craft.

Conceptualism was a single movement, however, and the art critic, looking across the art world, will say that she or he can see more techniques and crafts practised than ever before. The critic might contest my assertion that handicraft is disappearing as a major component of the plastic arts. Yet that same critic might also note that each individual tends to know only a little craft. Much less craft is understood by individuals than appears to be practised.

It is arguable that the diminution of craft knowledge and its status in the plastic arts is merely a part of a widespread phenomenon. After all, fragmentation of craft knowledge in the plastic arts appears to have a parallel in industry and modern technology, where different craft skills are held by individual people and become 'atomized'.

This comparison between industry and the art world is misleading, however. In industry we are seeing a redistribution of skills; but although individual members of a workforce may become less practically knowledgeable, industry as a whole retains as many or more skills than ever before. How can this be? Does it hold true for the plastic arts as well?

Bruno Latour, a philosopher and sociologist at the CSI-Ecole des Mines, Paris, has described the redistribution of skills in industry in an essay entitled 'Are we talking about skills or about the redistribution of skills?'[5] Latour begins with a simple example: the skill of measuring small amounts of liquid precisely into a container in laboratory conditions. In the recent past, a pipette might have been used similar to the kind used for administering medicinal eye or nose drops. Manual pipetting is difficult to repeat with precision, and in university and commercial laboratories such work would once have been given to skilled technicians. Students, too, would learn manual pipetting. However, the need to acquire this skill has been replaced by pipetting machines. Students need not bother with an obsolete craft, and technicians can be retrained.

The question is whether this change entails an increase or decrease in skill. The student remains unskilled; the technician's skills waste away. But the machine had to be designed, built and tested, all stages that require practical knowledge.

Other practical skills are brought about by this pipetting machine: it has to be brought from the factory to a laboratory, perhaps thousands of miles away; there are packagers, packaging designers, salesmen, transporters and methods of transport. It must also be maintained or repaired. From its conception through to its general use in laboratories, this machine represents a big increase in skill. It is an example of how the division of labour results in the redistribution of skill – it gives an undergraduate the ability to get on with his chemistry despite his lack of skill with a pipette.

Against the cornucopia of gains represented by replacing a manual skill with a machine, there is also a loss incurred. If the student is to become a practical experimenter – a constructor as well as a designer of laboratory experiments – then gaining knowledge of how to use a pipette machine accurately (which involves judgment and dexterity) might be regarded as a useful, transferable skill. It might be advantageous to learn to do things by hand even if a machine is available. The loss of the skill to the individual, moreover, has a social impact.

Consider industrial design and manufacturing. Teams of people work to produce a common goal: motor cars, for instance. The craft knowledge involved in the various stages of design and production may be progressively lost to individual workers whose skills are replaced by machines which may achieve the same results to a higher standard. Craft knowledge becomes distributed among the hardware and software of machines and computers. However, in one form or another a body of knowledge – the making of motor cars – is held intact. Indeed, it may be enhanced and deepened.

With regard to the plastic arts it is possible to argue that because of the diversity of different styles and movements, there are more ideas, techniques and knowledge in the art world than ever before. This is the conclusion offered by Anna Moszynska in her book *Abstract Art*: 'far from playing a reductive role, abstract art has greatly increased the range of ideas, techniques and materials open to all kinds of artists. This has obviously been the case throughout most of the twentieth century, and with the benefit of hindsight, its particular contribution is now becoming easier to assess.'[6] This argument is misleading. Craft knowledge is not open to all kinds of artists unless they work to attain it. What is transparent about contemporary art is that it is fragmented into a succession of diverse styles – there is no longer a body of craft knowledge shared by artists. Craft knowledge is becoming 'atomized'.

It can be argued that artists have access to a variety of fragmented skills inasmuch as they can delegate all the making of their art to others. But this argument presents the bizarre, unrealistic picture of an art object going from workshop to workshop having components added to it as if it were on a post-modern production line. Occasionally this happens, but not often, and where it does happen the artist has put himself or herself into the role of designer. Designers lose control over their creation once they relinquish it to production, whereas one of the strengths of a handicraft-based art form (see Chapter Five, pp. 80-3 and Chapter Six, pp. 101-4) is the flexibility it allows for the artist to change, expand and explore his original intention (or design) until the point he or she considers that the art work is complete.

Skill in industry is distributed systematically across a network of people, hardware and software. This system exists for the completion of a shared goal, such as the manufacture of cars. The plastic arts, on the contrary, are individualistic, competitive and not characterized by shared goals. There is no technology, no hard- or software for capturing and distributing the craft of art. If it is not acquired in substantial 'lumps' and passed on from person to person in a system of apprenticeship then it is lost. The rate of this loss increases the more the emphasis is put on the acquisition of mere segments of skill.

David Sweet, a British painter and art teacher, in an essay titled 'Towards a Militant Academy', has discussed the importance that is now given to style in art – a particular concern since the late nineteenth century: 'Schematization and fragmentation are the main agents of stylistic change ... Style identity springs from a decision to concentrate on a small section of the available options to the exclusion of others.'[7]

Such specialization can, of course, be a route to fruitful, creative expertise but if the specialism is not to collapse into a private, almost autistic enterprise then it needs to exist within a framework broader than itself.

Let us take an example outside the arts. A specialist in thermoplastics would be expert in a narrow body of knowledge, but within a broader framework of chemistry and materials technology. The connections between the specialism and the wider framework are not only theoretical but palpable – they are empirical. The specialist's language, methodology and craft may be tacitly understood by other chemists or materials engineers, even though they are not specialists in thermoplastics.

In the visual arts it is now rare to find a specialist who possesses broad skills which can be broadly applied. The artist who is competent in sculpting figuratively, painting, book illustrating and producing prints is an oddity. Competence here refers to the possession of the tacit knowledge that gives the artist a mental, conceptual and imaginative grasp of what can be done with and through each of these media. The emphasis upon competence is the important distinction. Many contemporary artists move from discipline to discipline but without acquiring much of the knowledge that once distinguished such disciplines.

Henri Matisse's career between 1869 and 1954 is worth considering here. In 1891, having resigned his job as a clerk in a lawyer's office, he enrolled in the Académie Julian in order to prepare for the entrance examination of the Ecole des Beaux-Arts. He left the Académie Julian in 1892 for evening classes at the Ecole des Arts Décoratifs and to study in the studio of Gustave Moreau, painter of detailed Biblical and mythological fantasies, whose tolerant, intelligent teaching at the Ecole des Beaux-Arts was highly valued. Matisse studied with Moreau off and on until Moreau's death in 1898. In 1899 he began intermittent study with the portraitist Eugène Carrière. In the late 1890s, he appears to have 'discovered' Impressionism. In 1898 he visited London and studied the paintings of J. M. W. Turner. In 1899 he became a convert to Pointillism: this is the theory and practice of optical mixtures. It is argued that brighter secondary colours can be obtained on a canvas not by mixing primaries on the palette but setting the primaries down as individual dots on the canvas. To obtain the secondary colour green, a painter usually mixes yellow and blue on the palette, but by intermingling separate dots of blue and yellow on the canvas and viewing the canvas from a certain distance, the colours 'mix' in the observer's eye. The disadvantage of this technique is that its innate rigidity tends to force all paintings using it into a strait-jacket of stylization. Matisse also studied the work of painters who worked in other manners: for example, he bought a painting by Paul Cézanne, another by Paul Gauguin and a drawing by Vincent van Gogh. In 1899 he began to attend an evening class in sculpture.

In 1905, working with André Derain and encouraged by Pointillism, Matisse began using freer colours and harsh combinations of complementaries: red against green, orange against blue, and yellow against violet. He was not alone in this; other painters were experimenting with colour in a similar manner. This manner of painting, later known as Fauvism, led some painters into Expressionism. Matisse developed a more controlled, decorative content influenced by a close study of nature, his continuing studies from the nude model, his training in the Western tradition of Renaissance and post-Renaissance art and an interest in Near Eastern art, especially in pattern-making. It is said that an exhibition of Near Eastern art held in Munich in 1910 stimulated his interest in flat patterns with arabesques and floral backgrounds. At the same time he was also working as a figurative sculptor, and although between about 1914 and the early 1920s he neglected sculpture, he returned to it in the late 1920s.

Throughout his career Matisse also pursued etching, drypoint, lithography and book illustration, as well as designing the sets and costumes for Sergey Diaghilev's production of *Le Chant du Rossignol* in 1920. In the 1940s Matisse produced many deceptively simple figurative paintings such as the *Deux Fillettes, Fond Jaune et Rouge* series. Among Matisse's last works were cut-out gouaches of decorative charm and simplicity. The French poet Louis Aragon, one of Matisse's biographers, wrote that these paper cut-outs crowned Matisse's work.

Today, however, in the spirit of specialization, and with art regarded in terms of linear progress, the modern student is most likely to eschew all the work that preceded Matisse's last works and to begin his or her own career by 'studying' the art of creating semi-abstract paper cut-outs, and thereafter trying to extend his or her own art from that small base. Moreover, the contemporary student will do this without the broader framework of craft knowledge that Matisse himself acquired as a student.

Today's student might be misled even more by the Matisse paintings of the 1940s (which preceded the cut-outs) whose spontaneity, ease and directness of line, extreme simplicity of form and bright yet limited colour appear to present easy victories for the aspiring student who does not want, for example, the slog of painting four still-lifes a day in order to learn tonal painting. Additionally, the apparently straightforward techniques – the lack of detail in the Matisse figures – appear to offer an easy way into a style. The student will be further encouraged by experts on Matisse, such as Patrick

Heron, who has written that Matisse demonstrates how 'stupid' and 'simplistic' are descriptive rules such as 'all reds advance; all blues recede'. Heron, looking at Matisse's late work, concludes 'there are no generalizations, no general truths about the illusionistically spatial operation of flat colours organized side by side across a flat surface.'[8]

Heron may be right, although his taste for hyperbole may have taken him too far. The crucial question, however, is how much a student can learn from Matisse. To gain access, as a practitioner, to the lessons implicit in Matisse's work it is surely the case that one needs to know the weight of rules, such as 'all reds advance, all blues recede', to set them aside. To gain access to Matisse's achievement demands practical knowledge. That practical knowledge cannot be inferred by looking at Matisse's work, the student must 'do' as well as look. One of the fundamentals of craft knowledge is that studying examples of it helps a student only in the context of practical teaching and demonstration. Merely to mimic late Matisse is not to grasp or absorb Matisse's knowledge.

Matisse belongs to a handicraft tradition in art that has been rendered almost defunct, partly as a consequence of the radical change in the nature of 'art's objects'. Any meaning that a Matisse painting or sculpture has is a result of craft knowledge: the thinking and making are soluble one with the other. With the transfer of art from a craft-based to a theory-based discipline, the objects of contemporary art stand as cyphers for theory: instead of being an expression, the contemporary art object is a representation of an idea.

Paintings, sculptures and other forms of plastic art can of course be about ideas. In Chapter Five, for example, reference will be made to the conceptual, emotional and empirical complexity of a painting by the seventeenth-century Dutch artist Judith Leyster. Moreover, the history of Western fine arts abounds in examples of work which include conceptual content and which connect with the network of contemporary ideas and issues. But my point concerns the relationship between the work of art and how it conveys or expresses ideas and whether or not the ideas gain by being expressed in art. This argument will become clearer with the help of an illustration. Pierre Degen is an artist from Switzerland, resident in London, famous in Europe in the early 1980s as an avant-garde jeweller, then as a performance artist and more recently as a constructivist or installation sculptor. His work has explored political themes. One such piece, shown in London in 1993, was called *Bread.* It was a tall structure, like a skeletal wigwam made from seven rods. The bottom half of each rod was wood, and each top half was metal. Each of the seven metal shafts speared a loaf of bread. Each loaf was high up, out of the reach of a tall adult. This, it was explained in the accompanying catalogue, represented denial of food; and the fact that there were seven loaves on seven staves was described in connection with the mythology of the number seven: seven days of the week, seven deadly sins and seven samurai. (Other modern cultural associations with the number seven such as the Seven Dwarfs or 7-Up were not, apparently, applicable.) The associations with the mythology of the number seven were cited in the catalogue as adding meaning to the piece. The work as a whole was summarized thus: '*Bread* is a comment on the inequalities of a society where many are still denied the "staff of life".'[9]

Although this example was chosen as a caricature of the 'object as cypher' style, it does reveal how art objects can become secondary to what is said about them. We can expose the workings of this trend further with a brief discussion of what is meant when it is claimed that a work of art represents an idea, person or a emotion as distinct from expressing it.

The following example comes from a lecture on the nature of representation in art given in 1971 by a British philosopher and aesthetician, Andrew Harrison.[10] He gave his lecture standing at a table beneath a hanging lamp and he made use of objects around him to illustrate his argument. He took an ashtray and told us that for the purposes of his illustration we were to understand that this ashtray represented the Pope. He then said, 'And I'd like this lamp hanging above me to be taken as representing the divine light of God.' He then put the ashtray directly under the light. Thus the Pope was in direct contact with God's divinity. Harrison next picked up an empty wastepaper bin, upended it and placed it over the ashtray. The wastepaper bin, said Harrison, represented the Cardinals and all the other advisers surrounding the Pope. The whole assemblage could then be described as symbolizing 'The Pope cut off from divine inspiration by the ignorance of his earthly advisers'. As a representation of an idea, the ashtray, lightbulb, wastepaper bin – together with the explanation – works at the level of language. In terms of plastic, three-dimensional art, however, it is aesthetically and artistically arbitrary.

Almost any object or part of an object can be put into an assemblage and be described as representing anything that assembler cares to say it represents.

What is missing is a congruity between the form and the representation. There is no necessary connection between the medium and the message. It is arguable that much contemporary art, especially installation art, works at this level – the words provide the content and the artefacts are merely pegs. Naturally, in such circumstances, craft knowledge is of secondary or even minimal importance.

On the contrary, expression may rely on a craft to work. Moreover, the essence of the expression cannot be caught in words – what the representation 'means' is in the craft, not what is said about it. The Italian painter Giorgio Morandi (1890-1964) spent much of his career painting still-lifes of relatively simple compositions of groups of bottles and vases. Morandi's paintings are austere and could be described as withdrawn and thoughtful. Some people may find it possible to infer from the work some spiritual quality.

The individual observer will bring to Morandi's still-lifes – as to any work of art (or science, for that matter) – his or her own assumptions and associations. However, there are common-sense limitations to this process of association. Were a critic to insist that he or she thought that Morandi was painting coded 'messages' about the Vatican, the muddle of Italian politics or a critique of the Italian bourgoisie, then a dozen other critics would ask for proof in the paintings to support such claims.

They might argue that although it was reasonable to 'see' domesticity, solace, quietness or stillness, there are no grounds for appropriating the paintings to fit very different theories of one's own. Moreover, whatever emotional, spiritual or other values are inferred from the paintings, Morandi was a master of the craft of painting still-lifes.

The craft of still-life painting is immensely rich: it is a 'language' of its own, independent of the language of words. What Morandi shows us cannot be expressed in words because the value of his work derives from his tacit knowledge.

From his tacit knowledge Morandi would recognize

- the local colour of each object
- the tone or value of each object
- the loss of local colour induced by the position of each object
- the interplay of shadows
- realism, harmony and emotion in terms of colour.

Morandi's paintings are examples of that practical knowledge. Not to know any of these elements would have reduced him to chance success.

Morandi and Matisse present pitfalls for the unwary contemporary artist or student of art. Such is the spontaneity with which both men paint, albeit in very different ways, that it is easy for those ignorant of the craft to consider the subject matter and style simple. For artists who produce aesthetically complex work, such as Vermeer, Chardin, Rodin, Matisse, Morandi, Lucian Freud, or for accomplished, knowledgeable studio crafts practitioners such as letterers, domestic potters or metalsmiths, the craft process inevitably becomes part of the subject matter. This interdependency of process and subject matter is discussed at length in Chapter Five.

Visual works that are aesthetically and conceptually complex are virtually impossible for individuals to create once their craft knowledge becomes atomized.

There is an important caveat to this discussion of the fragmentation of craft skill in the plastic arts. It can be argued that a relatively complete body of handicraft knowledge in painting continues within the 'Sunday Painting' movement. Amateur painters attend evening classes and summer schools in an effort to learn the craft of representational painting. And it may be argued that the network that feeds the amateur painter – the network of extramural, part-time tuition and amateur art societies – is sustaining the craft of painting. However, if credence is given to this view then it must be said that the sustenance is of a low order of quality – and that it is declining. This is not because to be amateur necessarily means low quality but because the quality of the knowledge being passed on through the extramural network is itself poor and declining. However, with an improvement in the training of art teachers the situation for amateurs could be reversed. I am also intrigued by the possibility that in the future the word 'crafts', which in the West currently refers to handicrafts such as ceramics or weaving and which, fairly or not, carries the association of 'amateurism' as distinct from fine arts 'professionalism', might also come to include in its definition painting, carving and modelling.

As it is, the effects of the fragmentation of skill knowledge and the substitution of tacit knowledge with theory are by no means so marked in the studio crafts as they are in the fine arts. The studio crafts, unlike the fine arts, contain the notion of service – the production of things that are beautiful and useful, or decorative in a way that is comprehensible to a large number of people. In the last twenty years, however, more and more craft practitioners have sought to concentrate on individualistic work, making use of very limited techniques and turning to art theory for meaning and legitimization of their work.

Within the applied arts four distinct practices may be identified. They are Functional, Representational, Figurative, and Self-referential.

Functional craft is designed for practical use. Industrial production has not made the applied artist redundant as a producer of functional items because a consumer market exists for well-designed, handmade, useful items, especially in ceramics, glass and furniture.

Representational craft is a category that includes all kinds of craft objects that resemble objects but whose aim is to be decorative. For example, numerous potters worldwide produce large and impractical jugs or bowls. They aspire to sculpture while keeping the look of a familiar object: they are a domestic art.

Figurative crafts include all forms of figure and animal and nature studies in two and three dimensions. Self-referential crafts are those objects made in, say, glass, wood, cloth or clay that are neither functional or figurative, nor do they represent anything – they are art objects whose meaning needs further elaboration in a catalogue or a caption. On the other hand it is in this category that one also finds (especially in glass or ceramics) objects that are abstract and sculptural and have no encoded 'meaning'.

The applied arts may also be (and more commonly are) divided by material or function: pottery, glassware, furniture, jewellery and so forth. Each of these areas has created its own avant-garde over the last twenty years.

A growing number of applied artists have a disparaging attitude towards craft knowledge. Alison Britton, a thoughtful British ceramicist with an established European reputation, is sceptical about the importance of craft knowledge. Britton is one of a handful of women ceramicists to have emerged during the 1970s in London (most graduated from the Royal College of Art) whose semi-abstract, constructed clay vessels (not thrown on the wheel) encouraged many more potters to produce 'sculptural', non-functional wares. Over the years her pots have become more abstracted – they are built from slabs of clay decorated with broad, rough brushstrokes of colour. They can be described as architectural, expressionist and rough.

In 1991 Britton was commissioned by the Crafts Council in London to write a catalogue essay for an exhibition about craft skill called *Beyond the*

Dovetail which I curated. She is a noted teacher and writer and I was keen to have her views put forward in the catalogue because we disagree. Here is a summary of that essay, entitled 'The manipulation of skill on the outer limits of function'.[11]

According to Britton, manual and mental skills are 'seamlessly combined' and the acquisition of practical skills 'to achieve the chosen ends is usually fairly straightforward'. For her, the 'hard part' is acquiring a sense of purpose and discovering what is worth making.

She thinks there is too much virtuoso work that has skill but no thinking: 'the virtuoso twiddles without the guts or sense of place'. Noting that some makers get bogged down in craft techniques, she asserts that the main responsibility of the artist craftsperson is 'the skilful achievement of relevance.'[12]

Function and utility, the core of craft work in the period before the Industrial Revolution, no longer provide that relevance. Britton believes that crafts are, like art itself, useless – mass production and the industrial designer have made it irrelevant for the craft movement to hold on to function as the core of its work. She maintains that because technology gives us smooth finishes, it is part of craft's oppositional role to adopt the rough aesthetic.

Craft skills, she suggests, are no longer 'relevant'. Picasso could draw well conventionally but later abandoned that skill. She, too, had learned to throw but found it an unnecessary skill for her purposes. She also describes some of the techniques of glazing her pots and offers these up as skills.

Britton speaks for many artists in the applied arts on both sides of the Atlantic when she says that the artist craftsperson is like the contemporary artist, and that the artist's path is 'a search for freshness, for alternatives, new angles'.[13]

In wondering why some observers are uncomfortable with modern craft Britton concludes that it unsettles people because it is not clear what it is about. Her own pots, she says, are barely representational. She does not know what the goals of her pots are and she is just struggling on the track of what is 'vivid and worth making' – every pot is, she hopes, another step on that track. She finds taking 'risks' pleasurable and has an 'anxiety' about not overworking her pots.[14]

Although I agree with her view that manual and mental skill should be combined, much of what she says is contentious: her argument, for example, that skills are easily acquired once the goals are set.

One of the fixed ideas about modern art education and art theory is that skills can be learned when they are needed – as if craft knowledge can be taken down from a supermarket shelf. However, this piece of modern received wisdom is seldom put to the test by those who preach it. The evidence weighs against Britton; eminent 'thinker-practitioners' have argued that tacit knowledge, the knowledge of practical thinking, is hard-won, even for the talented. John Ruskin, writing about drawing wrote, 'Do not, therefore, think that you can learn drawing, any more than a new language, without some hard and disagreeable labour.'[15]

Jan Gordon, explaining how one comes to understand the principles of tone in painting, all but recommends a diet of four still-life paintings a day for several months and a session of memory training.[16] Lucian Freud said, 'I remember everything I've done because it was done with difficulty.'[17]

Britton's thinking about skill has, I believe, been misled by the confusion, rampant in late twentieth-century discussions about craft, between possessing a small number of techniques as distinct from having a complex body of craft knowledge.

Simple techniques do not constitute a developed, articulated body of craft knowledge. A great many artists of the late twentieth century, be they in applied or fine arts, confuse craft knowledge with the acquisition of a relatively straightforward fabrication technique.

Britton's comparison with Picasso was misplaced. During his lifetime Picasso provided a good deal of evidence of his mastery of his discipline, and it is a moot point as to a) whether anyone understands what Picasso was doing in many of his later experiments and b) how much his experimentation was possible due to his complete mastery of a huge body of practical knowledge. One could argue that Picasso never discarded his knowledge and that it was the engine of his variety.

Nevertheless, Britton's strictures about the sterility (and vulgarity) of pursuing craft for craft's sake are, I believe, accurate – to an extent. This essay is not a defence of craft knowledge for its own sake, but rather as an alternative to propositional language and theory in order to articulate meaning in the visual arts. Nonetheless, as I make clear in the final chapter (see pp. 88-94), the automatic rejection of skill for skill's sake is a twentieth-century shibboleth which should not be accepted without question.

My purpose is not to decry contemporary developments in the plastic arts but to discuss the misconceptions that have developed about tacit knowledge.

3 Learning a Craft

A common assumption is that craft skills are mechanically learned and exercised; and that they are thus obviously unthinking and uncreative. This modern prejudice goes hand in hand with an attitude, perhaps peculiar to the latter half of the twentieth century in Western culture, that one can learn skills as and when one thinks one needs them. I think we have lost an understanding of what the learning of skills involves, especially in the plastic arts.

This chapter considers what the learning of skills entails and whether or not learning by rote and constant practice – which seems such a burden – constitute a long-term brake on expression and creativity.

Learning a skill is not the same as being expert. Being an expert in a body of craft knowledge means living that knowledge. The problem with being a beginner at a skill, or even at being 'pretty proficient', is that fluency in the body of knowledge cannot be taken for granted. This makes learning a skill a hard business: doing a skill badly when wanting to create something excellent is a demoralizing experience. This is why learning is not and cannot always be fun. Learning a skill is not a mechanical activity but an emotional as well as intellectual and physical process.

A second complication is that appearances are deceptive. Other people's skills, applied expertly, appear mechanical – without thought or the burden of having to work hard. Some apparently routine, repetitive tasks performed by artisans are not in fact mechanical – at least not in the machine-like sense. A characteristic of a machine, provided it is set or programmed properly, is that it is predictable and does not get distracted or bored, nor does it possess a 'will' to subjugate to the task in hand. People who perform mechanical tasks must normally call on considerable self-discipline.

For example, the French philosopher Simone Weil spent time working in a Renault car factory in 1936, and of this experience she wrote: 'In front of his machine, the worker has to annihilate his soul, his thought, his feelings, and everything, for eight hours a day. If he is irritated, or sad, or disgusted, he must swallow and completely suppress his irritation, sadness, or disgust; they could slow down his output.'[1]

This battle to subjugate oneself to the demands of mechanical work was one of the themes of an exhibition about industrial craft called *The Cutting Edge*, held at the Ruskin Gallery, Sheffield, in 1992. Sheffield was once one of the powerhouses of British manufacturing industry specializing in every kind of hand-held tool, blade and cutlery. Some of this work was still being done in the 'old way' (largely by hand, in small, unautomated workshops) in the 1960s. A local historian who knew the industry captured the work on film which he subsequently narrated, and recorded the comments of the men, many of whom he knew. Two aspects of this film are notable here.

First, almost all measurements taken during the making of a blade (small or large) were done by eye. The men had learnt to repeat this accurately – or so it seemed. Such a mythology surrounds all old-fashioned craft processes, that we assume that in those days a good craftsman was somehow superhuman, who did things by eye to perfection, never putting a stroke wrong and always working with an easy fluency.

Secondly, and more important, the men could be seen fighting themselves to maintain the rate of production and the accuracy of the repetition. Some swore all the time, cursing their material as they swung hammers to beat out blades, others were hatchet-faced and silent. They knew how to do their work but it remained a discipline that they forced out of themselves every day. The men 'policed' themselves constantly. This is far from machine-like, it is not 'merely mechanical'.[2]

What links the artisan and the artist in their ability to call on a body of craft knowledge, be it a number of techniques as in cutlery-making, or something more complex, such as portrait-painting, is the necessity at some stage of undergoing a period of training. Peter Gullers, a photographer, describes the general character of craft apprenticeship like this:

> Many people would like to acquire skills, but the long and arduous years of apprenticeship are a deterrent. To file pieces of metal day in and day out as engineering apprentices had to do, or to devote several hours a day to practising the movements of classical dance, may be compared to equestrian dressage. Both self-control and, to some extent, physical and intellectual subjection are needed.[3]

To enter by free choice into the discipline of learning affects your commitment. You do not then fight the learning procedures or treat them as a tyranny, you embrace their necessity. The commitment to learning is, in any case, goal-oriented. To do classical dance or portrait-head sculpture or mathematics, the knowledge that constitutes 'doing' those activities has to be acquired. What is important is the goal and the strength of the determination to meet it. Just wanting to be 'creative' is not, in itself, likely to be strong enough to sustain the will. It is necessary to want to do something specifically, be it portraiture or calligraphy or learning the piano. In deciding upon these goals one accepts the need to acquire the rules and conventions of the knowledge that constitute them. However, some artists and art students believe that the only purpose of a rule is to be questioned. Questioning convention is the orthodoxy of the avant-garde.

Rules are often thought of in terms of regulations. We accept that, for our well-being, or for the greater good of the community, some rules allow and some forbid. Inherent to the nature of society's prescriptive rules is their generality, their anonymous authority and the threat of a penalty if they are not fulfilled. They remain, however, external to our inner lives. They regulate us but they do not constitute us as individuals. A foreigner entering our community or our country can learn these rules quickly enough, with the help of a book and a good memory. Or to take another example, you need not be able to drive a car in order to understand the rules of the Highway Code.

But understanding the Highway Code is not the same as being able to drive a car. The Highway Code regulates but does not constitute driving cars. Constitutive rules are the sort of rules which can only be acquired or assimilated and thus fully understood by doing them. Reading about them barely helps. To understand the constitutive rules of a culture or a social class, for example, you have to 'go native'. We grow up with constitutive rules and grow into them. They exist in the interactions between people, in the nuances of voice, the stance of the body as well as in the content of the conversation. These constitutive rules do not regulate our behaviour: they actually are our behaviour. We learn them in our bones through being in the community with people like us; we absorb by mimicry much more than by being told. It is very hard for an outsider (a beginner) to 'go native': whether it be trying to fit in with another class of people, another profession or another country, the outsider is trying to absorb another culture, most of which is unspoken.

By analogy, when we learn a craft or any other discipline in which one wants to become expert, one is attempting to 'go native'. To learn a craft is to acquire the rules that constitute that craft's practice.

The constitutive rules of a craft are only learned by actually doing the activity. Indeed, they are the activity. This is a fundamental point about craft knowledge. You cannot understand it or know it until you can do it. Reading about it is not the same as understanding it. The philosophical basis of this point, which has implications for learning and teaching, was explored by Wittgenstein in *Philosophical Investigations* (1953): this is to be discussed in the next chapter.

To investigate this idea empirically I temporarily apprenticed myself (at different times) in two different disciplines: lettering and portrait-sculpture in clay.

Lettering is primarily a functional art. In recent years, especially as a result of developments among calligraphers and letterers in Germany, the USA and Britain, there has been an emphasis upon lettering as an expressive art in its own right. But whatever their professional inclinations, most practitioners agree that there is a craft to be learned through which the particularities of the function or the expression are discovered and created.

The same is almost true of portrait-sculpture. It is a functional art in that artists are commissioned to create a likeness of someone. It is also an expressive art insofar as it is possible to express certain characteristics of the sitter. The elements of 'likeness' and a 'sitter's character or presence' can be elusive.

The craft of both these arts is complex, rich and subtle. There are rules to learn and facts to acquire.

The lettering in which I was schooled was using pen and ink on paper. Other possibilities in lettering include brush, ink and paper or chisel and stone. The differences between the use of a nib, brushstrokes and carving are deliberation and physical action: carving a groove deliberately and methodically is different from drawing a pen nib down the page or sweeping around on paper with a brush. You cannot, for example, push a steel-nibbed pen without ploughing into the paper.

The portrait-sculpture to which I was introduced was of two kinds: modelling a solid head in clay, and modelling a hollow head in clay. Modelling in solid clay is easier than modelling a hollow head because of the 'engineering problems' of constructing a vessel that juts out into space at various places and whose thin surface has to be built. The advantages of a hollow head, however, are in the final processes. As my tutor Neal French explained, if the head is to be fired it has to be hollow. A solid head must be cut in half, the inside scooped out and the two halves fixed together. Inevitably the sculpture is damaged in the process and it must be reworked, thus lessening its 'freshness'.

In both crafts – lettering and portrait-sculpture – there are, as one would expect, many facts to learn and many of these concern the tools and the materials. But although there are exercises to practise in order to acquire some of the basic handling techniques, one more or less begins straight away by developing judgment and discrimination.

The issue of 'likeness' is important in both crafts. Lettering employs alphabets; alphabets are families of letters, they look alike. Each alphabet has its likeness and that likeness is conveyed throughout the alphabet; one has to catch it. In portraiture, capturing likeness is more complicated. In both crafts the achievement of likeness involves learning to discriminate in detail as well as the larger scale of general outline, shape or form. Surprisingly quickly, this discrimination involves connoisseurship. One begins to become aware of qualities of line, texture or form: qualities such as verve, life, deadness, or freshness.

Using words such as 'dead' or 'limp' or 'lively' to describe the success or failure of a line or a form introduces the student to a different set of criteria from those of construction. Criteria of construction concern such things as a line or a form being in the wrong place or being the wrong shape. However, understanding criteria of quality as well as criteria of construction is a sign that one is beginning to 'go native' in the craft.

Criteria of quality, for all their subjective, metaphorical character, are not judgments made on a whim. They have an objectivity: their objectivity is the substance of that craft's connoisseurship. To say that a line is 'dead' is to point to something objective even though the language one uses is metaphorical.

The beginner is concerned only with basic likeness and structural criteria. In calligraphy, the British beginner's alphabet is Edward Johnston's foundational hand. He based his alphabet on that used in a tenth-century Carolingian manuscript whose letters have a rounded, open quality.[4]

Ann Hechle, my lettering tutor, explained that Johnston's alphabet is based on the circle. As a teaching alphabet, the form of the circle gives an absolute goal on which both the teacher and the pupil can agree. Deviations are easily seen. A circle is hard to draw but relatively easy to hold in the mind as a mental template. If a letter or a part of a letter is based on the circle or a segment of the circle, then by recalling the circle form one knows what to draw (even if one is uncertain about how to draw it).

In the early stages there are basic problems, such as learning how to hold the pen at the correct angle relative to the page. The early stages can be described as copying and – to a degree – learning to draw Johnston's alphabet might seem much easier than learning to make a portrait head. But in fact, faced with the subtleties of the foundational alphabet, what seems like 'mere' copying is not. It is not much use simply trying to follow Johnston's lines. One must understand how the forms are constructed. This understanding is greatly helped by teaching and demonstration.

Johnston's letters are constructed from more than one part – the pen or brush must be lifted to complete the letter forms. The first stage in drawing the foundational alphabet is to practise drawing lines at an angle of 30 degrees because most of the letters are shaped by the pen nib being held at an angle of 30 degrees to the horizontal plane.

It helps to watch and then to mimic the élan with which the tutor draws the letter – mimicry and demonstration make the learning task much easier. The memory of movements made by someone else is a sort of jig to hold in the mind and use. Listening to an explanation of what the drawing of a letter O entails is not the same as actually understanding the rule of for drawing an Johnston's foundational O – that comes only through doing and from demonstration. I cannot be told what to do. I can be nudged, I can be shown and then I keep trying until I am following the rule of drawing the O, and the rule is embedded in the practice itself – it is not isolated from it.

The first homework was to draw the letters in ink at random without laying them out or spacing them. After my second lesson, where the homework from the first was reviewed, I noted that I had willed myself to understand Ann's criticisms of my letters, but could not honestly claim that I could see my mistakes.

Seeing mistakes, gaining the ability to discriminate, is the key to becoming an expert.

When I began to study portrait-sculpture with Neal French, I started with a solid clay blank (rather than attempting a hollow or vessel head straight off) to get a feel for some of the problems. Neal's advice was to establish the forehead first – being bony it does not move, and it is a datum point to which other, more mobile aspects of the face can be related. After the forehead one positions the cheek-bones and upper jaw.

I was told to take a good look at the model's head all round and to look at the relationship between the the back of the skull and its front, the back of the skull and the chin, and to look carefully at what shape is formed by the head and the neck at the back. I was told to look down on the head, from the back of the head, from three-quarters – trying to see the relationships between the main forms.

But I could see no such things: there was too much to look at and I did not know what I could ignore. It is very hard to describe this 'non-seeing': it does not mean literally being unable to see forms and shapes, it means not understanding them. Understanding means having the sense of their shape and weight in one's mind, recognizing the possibilities for editing and moving those shapes and forms for the purpose of making a representation.

One learns judgment through doing. I note from my lettering work diary,

> I have been writing out the alphabet. Most irritating is the fact that the two halves of the letter 'm' never seem to fit together. The arches rise too steeply or the spaces are not equal. The letters 'i' 'j' and 'l' are tricky because they are minimalist letters and they have to be set down 'just so'. At the moment I wobble and splatter.

An interesting complication about learning, however, concerns the mismatch between judgment and practical ability. Practical work is undoubtedly the major route to discrimination but discrimination can often outgrow ability. This can cause problems. For example, I recall having to write out a sentence with forty-seven words. I could barely get to the end of it. I had noted in the diary, 'I am having difficulty in completing a piece of work.' But a novice cannot scrap botched work without completing it first. In order to make progress one has to go through with each project to the end even though its many flaws are a reminder of one's incompetence.

It is not universally true that everyone finds the acquisition of such skills a battle. Different people have different aptitudes. Nevertheless, the discipline of finishing work that is not what you had hoped is hard for many people. It is not always the case that judgment is ahead of what one can practically accomplish. Sometimes you think you have done good work when you have not. I have in the past been shocked at how, having completed a drawing and thinking it quite good, I have discovered a few weeks later that it is really quite bad. What I saw then and what I see now are not the same.

However, in spite of the fact that judgment and practical ability are not always congruent, the very acquisition and practice of craft knowledge is woven in with judgment and ideas about what you are doing and learning. Practical work is not independent of your mental grasp of it: they are inextricably bound in with one another.

To draw a capital letter C to fit the lower case Johnston foundational alphabet, you are essentially trying to ensure that at both open ends of the

C the line is flattened away from the course that a true circle would take. This move away from a true circle creates the 'right' internal shape. There is no word for this 'right' internal shape (even if there was it would not help). The rightness or wrongness of the shape is something that one learns to recognize – it is a part of the connoisseurship and the practical ability of drawing letter Cs.

To make any kind of progress, some element of judgment and selection is involved – the very least that is required is an act of engagement on the part of the student. Some philosophers agree. For example, as Allan Janik has noted, in Wittgenstein's *On Certainty* one finds the radical educational idea that a teacher teaches the student everything he or she knows. But the student may not want everything she knows. To explain this point Janik uses the example of the ballet teacher, whom the pupil must watch and imitate, for it is only once the pupil has learned how to dance that the teacher can talk about further rules and styles.[5]

But in imitating the teacher the pupil has to make a judgment – to 'see' and copy what is relevant and not relevant. Learning to write Os, I recognized that it was helpful to imitate the way my teacher held the pen, her wrist movement, the placing of the wrist of her drawing hand upon the board, but not that she pursed her lips or squinted her eyes. We need to discern what is relevant and what is not.

When I spent time learning to sculpt portraits, I felt that the pupil may profit from mimicking much more than is strictly relevant about the way the master or mistress works. Standing like the master, adopting his mannerisms, acting like him in order to get at his knowledge, occurred to me as a plausible learning tactic. Students do model themselves on their teachers – and, if they are good students, they grow out of it. Judging what is relevant and not relevant takes time. Wittgenstein's observation – that we have to be discerning – reinforces the argument that learning is not passive: it demands the engagement of the pupil and the need for judgment.

In learning a craft, the role of mimicry is probably essential. This means one needs to work alongside a skilled practitioner. My teacher in portrait-sculpture worked from the same model that I did. The notion that skills are learned by working with skilled people is not restricted to the arts. The sociologist of science, Harry Collins, has formulated the notion into a general axiom: 'Skill-like knowledge travels best (or only) through accomplished practitioners.'[6]

It is essential the novice be presented with standards of work to strive towards. The goal has to be external. Progress in practical ability and judgment is an exchange, a continuous looking to and from what the pupil, the teacher and other expert practitioners have accomplished. It is in this exchange that the communal knowledge of the craft is teased out and parts of it are gradually made one's own.

As one learns and builds techniques, so the capacity to judge increases. But at the same time one is searching for recipes, for jigs, for schematic structures to help you make the 'right' decisions. Some of these jigs are discarded as you become more knowledgeable, others may retain their usefulness. Naturally the use of jigs, of schemas, of recipes, is two-edged. They provide you with a way into solving a problem, but they may also set your thinking in too rigid a pattern.

First, let me give an example of a jig or recipe. During the later stages of working on a hollow head portrait-sculpture under the direction of Neal French, I was running into problems with working out the right structure for the cheek-bones, the eye sockets and the mouth. The model had a distinctive mouth – it was especially severe in repose and if I could get the set of it right then I would be on the path to getting a better likeness overall. It was not until I had had a lesson in the anatomy of the mouth that I made any progress: the muscles around the mouth form a sort of circle which establishes the mouth.

I needed a similar lesson for the eyes. Neal took some clay and built me part of a face showing the nose, cheek-bone and eye. He built it up in simple forms – making a big arc for the bony part of the forehead, the top of the eye socket, and then built up a good rounded semi-sphere for the eyeball. Then he enclosed the top and bottom of the sphere with an arch for the upper lid and an arch for the lower lid, cleanly delineating the forms with a modelling tool. The result was not much like a real eye, but it was a good convention for an eye and a foundation for making an eye that would look like the model's.

Methods such as that just described are useful for providing the learner with a foundation. They are also useful as bridges for discussion: they bridge the gulf between the student's incomprehension and the teacher's knowledge. Teachers – whether they are teaching and demonstrating face to face or trying to pass on knowledge through the less satisfactory medium of writing books (or giving television or video lectures) – know much more than they can articulate. Moreover, they know more than they can realistically demonstrate although one of the benefits of the five- or seven-year apprenticeships in craft disciplines of old was that the apprentice picked things up by working, living and watching in a real workshop producing real work. That does not seem to be possible in the modern teaching studio.

Recipes, jigs and schema are thus very useful methods of condensing information and of providing a point of discussion between the student and the teacher. Part of a teacher's craft is knowledge of recipes and how to use them.

The usefulness of schema and recipes, however, is tempered by the possibility that they will encourage too narrow a way of looking at fresh problems. What begins as a useful learning and teaching strategy can harden into a trick or device to underpin superficial or meretricious work later on.

Tricks and devices were the theme of a paper given by the Dutch philosopher Guy A. M. Widdershoven at an international conference on skill in 1989, 'A Narrative Theory of Skill'. He said, 'The notion of skill is easily confounded with that of a trick which one is able to perform irrespective of one's further ideas and actions.'[7] If I understand him correctly then what Widdershoven means is that a trick can be performed almost automatically, without thinking about it. Further, that a trick is a self-contained act or artefact, complete in itself, which requires no further thought or development. And in art it is possible to accumulate a bag of tricks. There are various kinds: there are complete recipes or schemas such as those used by fashion illustrators, for example. These illustrators appear to have four or five stock figures in their head which they set down with near mechanical ease.

In drawing or watercolour painting there are many tricks for hiding or 'improving' a bad piece of work. Options such as rubbing out a substantial part of a drawing can rescue it because the resulting ambiguity allows the observer's brain to supply the missing information. Most techniques for rescuing drawings are to do with ambiguity – washing out, scumbling and fudging charcoal are examples. Tricks of ambiguity, which can be palmed off as expressionism, are found throughout the plastic arts.

The status of tricks is not clear-cut. Certainly they close down the mind, and they are indeed the basis of much superficial work. Yet, equally, most experts know many tricks. There are tricks that portrait painters have for painting eyes or getting the hair right – we call this style or even the 'unique signature' of the artist. We expect experts to have a 'few tricks up their sleeves', short cuts, means of getting the basics accomplished without having to re-invent the tradition of their discipline every time they embark on something new.

The fact that one can work within the comfort of an easily absorbed set of rules is not an argument against their usefulness. It is a matter of judgment – perhaps of moral will – whether or not the individual decides he or she wishes to make do or go further; it is a matter of moral will if one knows one's work is meretricious but decides to leave it in that state in the hope of getting away with it: then there is a loss of integrity. The temptation to opt for a collection of tricks, to learn a summary of a skill, not by mastering its complexities and nuances, but by acquiring a prècis of it through its schemas, is most attractive in the novice stage of learning.

The benefit for the novice of having a skilled practitioner to teach him is multifaceted. One advantage is that if one's teachers are themselves good artists then they cannot help but reveal to the novice the possibilities that exist for extending the craft, for putting recipes and techniques to use: in short, they cannot help demonstrate the principle of 'rules are there to be broken' (but only if you fully understand them in the first place).

A small example impressed me when I was learning capital letters with Ann Hechle. After I had made a hopeless hash of my first attempts she demonstrated the construction of the letters once again. I noticed, however, that when she drew the letter N the diagonal between the two uprights was not 'textbook straight'. Was the letter then botched? No. It was a nice looking N whose tautness derived from the way the diagonal line bowed slightly as though compressed between the two uprights. Therein lay the secret of its vitality. It was an example of the creative breaking of a rule and a successful departure from the standard recipe for doing that kind of letter N.

The purpose of acquiring skills is to put them to use; unless one's aim is limited to repeating the designs of other people, then one of the skills one needs is the ability to experiment. Experimenting, which is often described as playing around, itself demands judgment – it involves improving one's sense of discrimination. It may well be that one produces designs that are only 'good for me' (and no one else) but it still matters that one has an understanding of why it is good. Experimenting, even if it is regarded as play, is more than messing about. Messing about in an unstructured way no doubt has its uses, like yielding useful accidents, but one develops one's discriminatory skills more readily within a structure.

That structure can be flexible, tolerant and liberal – it is the structure of knowledge represented by the teacher who, having greater, deeper access to a body of knowledge, can point to interesting developments or simply ask pertinent questions about the student's play.

It is easier to describe what is meant by this by referring to back to the learning of lettering. Once you begin putting letters into words and words into sentences then you become concerned with the texture of lettering. Texture depends partly on the weight of individual letters and their serifs, still more on the internal spacing between letters, spacing between words and spacing between lines. Some letters take up more space than others and some combinations of letters look better than others. What one is often looking for in a word or a line of words is an even distribution of light and dark. A word should neither look full of gaps, nor should it present itself as a black hole in a line of writing. There are occasions where, for the sake of expressing the sense of a word, one chooses to break a rule. An example could be a line of poetry such as this exceptionally odd line from William Blake's poem 'The Clod and the Pebble': 'So sung a little Clod of Clay'. If one sought in drawing those words to capture the forms that are described by the words 'sung', 'little', 'clod' and 'clay', one might have a variation in height, in spacing, and in light and dark, thus breaking conventions about even distribution of light and dark.

Generally, when writing out a text, the goal is to get bands of text emerging across the page such that, when one looks at the page as a piece of text, it is not riven, like a piece of limestone rock, with crevices and rivulets of white space breaking up the text. The eye will pounce on these rivulets of text and follow them down the page with the consequence that one's desire to read the text from left to right is constantly interrupted by these diverting fork lightning shafts of white paper.

It was at this stage, when I was experimenting with short pieces of text, that the distinction between readability and legibility began to have some consequence for my exercises. In *Letters of Credit*, a book concerning the design of type, the author, Walter Tracey, makes a distinction which at first can seem niggling but which, applied to hand-drawn lettering, is quite important.[8] He says that legibility refers to individual letters and that readability refers to how long one may read (and comprehend) a piece of text without tiring. I noted earlier that in lettering one can, indeed should for the sake of the word, sacrifice individual letters by running them into one another so that they touch or even become joined. This is especially the case with awkward combinations of letters such as lower case pairs like these: ae/ ra/ ri/ rv/ tt/ ff/ fl/ th. One can do this because the reader is familiar with the words and the meaning of the word makes up for the ambiguity of some of its visual parts.

Familiarity apart, spacing between letters and between words is an important aspect of readability – as maintained by hundreds of letterers and type designers.

Ann Camp, calligrapher and author of a basic guide to learning lettering, *Pen Lettering*, says – along with most letterers – that capital letters cannot be spaced properly simply by allowing the same measurement between each of them. If it is decided that every letter in a word should be, say, 1mm apart, the result will be an uneven appearance of white space. Getting the spacing right between words and letters is a subtle business. Even measurement gives uneven appearances. Spacing then is done 'by eye'.[9]

But what does this mean? It does not mean giving up on measurement altogether. The A demands equal areas of white above and below the bar. Likewise, each V of white space in the letters M and W should be equal in area. In placing letters together the aim is to get an even spread of white within the word as a whole and some letters have to be closer together on account of their shape than others. This is best done 'by eye'. It is a skill which demands a sensitivity to the creation of white shapes between letters – it is a matter of design, of getting a feeling for the balance between light and dark, but it is not, in essence, mysterious. There are general rules. Camp says:

a) two uprights should be far apart – so that the area of width is 'rather less than the width of the letter H'.
b) An upright and a curve should be rather closer.
c) Two curves should be closer still – 'almost touching so that the areas of white between these two letters will appear optically to be the same as between two uprights'.[10]

Implicit in these general rules is the characteristic 'vagueness' that one finds in cooking recipes. The vagueness is not confusion or ambiguity but a recognition that the actual fitting together of the components is up to the individual's perception and experience.

After a while, having satisfied Ann Hechle that I understood some of the principles of spacing, she set up some lessons in which I was to experiment with spacing, meaning, design and layout. The first exercise required me to think about the placing on the page of a short piece of poetry. The words were:

Now sleeps the crimson petal, now the white.

There are many ways that these words can be arranged on a page – in a circle, in the shape of a petal, diagonally, in a list going down the page, or as a spiral. In fact, it seemed sensible and right just to put them down as straightforwardly as possible because the language itself is distinctive and there is no point in interfering with the quietness of the metaphor. The rhythm of the line is sonorous and one can imagine the writer trying out different combinations.

Simply reversing the colours ruins the line:

Now sleeps the white petal, now the crimson.

However, it is at this point that the novice gets a glimmer of the calligrapher's art: here one enters into graphic design, balancing the meaning of the words with a design on the page. The extent to which a calligrapher/designer should impose his or her art on someone else's work is a matter of judgment.

I thought that the only embellishment the words demanded was the sonorous rhythm of the foundational hand and a rhythm of white spaces that at no point got in the way of that of the words themselves. However, as an exercise it fell to me to experiment.

One obvious arrangement is to put the words on two lines:

Now sleeps the crimson petal ,
now the white.

This seems to bludgeon the meaning home, as do other variations:

Now sleeps the crimson petal,
now the white.

or

Now sleeps the crimson petal,
now the white.

Writing it here, at a keyboard, I am avoiding all the other issues of composition which can arise and which will include the choice of alphabet. I can only draw in the foundational hand, but a skilled letterer may isolate key words or, at the very least, find a hand that looks right for the quiet closing up of the flowers. And, of course, there is colour. Would it be very vulgar to use black, crimson and white on grey paper? It could be interesting to find out.

Less complicated options demanding the letterer or designer's eye concern the physical placement of the words amidst all the white of the page. How wide should the margins be?

Ann went over an exercise she used with other students. It depends on being able to draw two alphabets – the foundational and compressed – and in this (long) lesson I received a crash course in the compressed lettering.

Ann Hechle's text, which began 'Noah sends forth the dove ...', consisted of a heading, a main text and the two footnotes giving chapter and verse. She had prepared the body of text but the heading and footnotes she made available in a variety of sizes. She then posed two questions:

a) Which is the best size of heading and footnote for the text?
b) Where do you place these elements on the page?

The best size of heading and footnote depends on the use that is to be made of the text. Is it to be included in a book or used as a notice board, a sign or a poster? The context of function sets up a variety of criteria – from how far away is the composition to be read? From how far away does it have to be noticed? There are related questions, such as whether the piece overall is intended to be 'decorative', 'utilitarian' or somewhere in between the two. A decorative piece means that both legibility and readability can drop down in the hierarchy of importance, but not out altogether since the sense of the text provides the decoration with its existence and its justification.

In lettering there is a lot of scope for decoration. One uses the pen as an instrument of drawing, and Ann Hechle, for example, enjoys creating flourishes that make a word lift and fly. A sentence beginning 'Noah sends forth the dove' is a good opportunity for creating a design that conveys the expansiveness of the scene. It is a challenge for graphic design which has to be approached with as much thought as possible about the compositional and functional criteria. One can, for example, bind the words into a knot with the word 'dove' being set free.

Ann's composition of the Noah text on paper was interesting. In order to experiment quickly one may photocopy the texts, cut them up and play with them on the page. We are looking all the time at both sense and formality.

That is to say, the integrity of the meaning conveyed by the words must be respected, while at the same time the layout must be organized according to the goals we have set. Is the goal to enhance the meaning of the words? Is it to create a calligraphic artefact in which the words are an excuse for calligraphic art? – and so on.

The playing around with composition is not as arbitrary as the phrase would indicate. There are rules in composition which, though not binding, do affect the final look and usefulness of design.

Here is one such rule: white space bleeds black line or black mass of its intensity. Too much white space between words or lines, or too big a margin around a piece of text, or at the top and bottom of the page, will kill off the vibrancy of the line. Too little white will increase the darkness and make the text appear knotted up. It ought to be an easy rule to see but it is not. I am not a connoisseur of light/dark relationships in text and layouts.

Ann explained that, broadly speaking, one has the choice between a centred and an asymmetrical design. What one does not normally have is the option of combining the two conflicting approaches. Because the eye is generally searching for a coherent pattern (because we are trying to make sense of what we see) then a conflict in the overall strategy of a composition will be uncomfortable because the brain cannot resolve the two opposing patterns.

One of the things that can go wrong for the beginner, as I found out, is the accidental occurrence of unintended patterns in a composition. You have to keep an eye on the particular, the local and the overall aspects of your design to check what white or black patterns have appeared.

This was more or less as far as I went with the lettering exercise. To make progress I would have had to keep practising the foundational alphabet and the capital letters and gradually acquire other alphabets as well. Were I to do this then the time would come when I could devise my own variations, perhaps even my own alphabet. I had reached a stage where I now understood what I was going to have to do to become even halfway competent as a letterer, let alone to make an 'art' out of it.

The conclusions that I draw are not scientific: they are not the product of many individuals with control groups providing benchmarks against which to measure inferences. Nonetheless I believe they are useful in a contemporary discussion of the worth of craft skill; some will strike the reader more obviously than others:

a) Acquiring a body of practical knowledge takes time: it is a slow empirical process. Intellectual leaps via theoretical insights are useful, but only after practice. Conceptualization about craft means much more to the practitioner than to the non-practitioner. This is because the rules that make up practical knowledge – the constitutive rules – cannot be apprehended intellectually until one begins to be able to do them. Naturally, some people with talent or aptitude can acquire some skills very quickly, just as some have an aptitude for mathematics or philosophy.
However, because skill knowledge – at its more profound level – tends to be open-ended, then to be gifted at a discipline means also that you are faced with extending it to a higher level than someone who is more or less a duffer. Everyone is likely to face problems but the level and complexity of those problems vary from individual to individual.

b) For most people, in most crafts, I would argue that knowledge has to be passed on from skilled person to novice. There are many ways in which this happens. However, it is also the case that some people can infer the essentials of a craft from past examples. Traditionally, most painters and sculptors studied work from the past (and from their peers) to learn new ways of doing things. However, they also worked in studios with other people, attended academies or worked in an extended community in which similar ideas and processes to their own were worked out.

c) There is a great difference between acquiring a small number of tricks and acquiring a grasp of a body of practical knowledge. You can acquire fragments of skill; but if you limit yourself to the techniques, then you may forfeit expertise in a variety of skills within the same discipline. With portrait-head sculpture, for example, one may learn how to do a nose or an eye, but to learn the bone structure and the position of muscles will provide you with more flexible skills when faced with the goal of individual likeness.

d) Recipes are useful in the process of learning a skill; they are useful in the exercise of expertise; but they become handicaps if they constitute the entirety of one's practical knowledge.

e) The interdependency of content and process, it is soon learnt, is not a mechanical procedure. It involves discrimination, and judgment. Discrimination is an intellectual ability that has to go hand in hand with practical learning – otherwise you do not know what you are doing and can make no purposeful improvements.

f) Practical know-how is a spur to conceptual reflection: it prompts questions such as 'what happens if I try it this way?' Such questions, however, imply that you have a choice: that choice is only earned by intelligent studentship.

4 Do Experts Follow Rules?

From the last chapter it will be obvious to any skilled artist that I had only begun to scratch at the surface of either of the crafts discussed; moreover, some of the difficulties I describe can be put down to my lack of talent rather than the intrinsic difficulty of acquiring graphic or sculptural knowledge. Unfashionable though it is to say, some people have a natural disposition towards practical work that the rest of us lack. Whether these differences are the result of nature or nurture is not a matter for discussion here. Clearly having a talent for something makes learning easier but it does not remove the necessity for having access to the relevant bodies of knowledge. In the arts under discussion in this essay, this means the individual needs to acquire a body of knowledge, mentally and physically.

Many people have considered the issue of talent. One of the most interesting brief discussions of talent is given in Richard Rees's biography of Simone Weil, in which Rees agrees with Weil that talent and genius, and talent and intellect are separate entities. Rees writes of Weil, 'it may be true that her natural facilities did not include any very special or remarkable talents, but only a brilliant and powerful intellect which, like all intellect, can be compared to a machine. Intellect can help a man to develop his talents, but it is not itself a talent.'[1]

Another brief discussion worth noting is provided by G. H. Hardy, one of this century's most important pure mathematicians. In *A Mathematician's Apology*, Hardy writes, 'perhaps five or even ten per cent of men can do something rather well. It is a tiny minority who can do anything really well ... if a man has any genuine talent, he should be ready to make almost any sacrifice in order to cultivate it to the full.'[2]

Hardy discovered a mathematician even more brilliant than himself – Srinivasa Ramanujan (1887-1920). Most of what Ramanujan knew about mathematics (which, it is said, was a startling amount) was discovered by himself. However, there were also surprising gaps in his knowledge. And according to C. P. Snow, who knew Hardy well, Hardy believed Ramanujan to be a creative mathematician of the first class, but defects in his education meant that his contribution was not as great as it could have been.[3]

The moral is obvious: even the greatest talent benefits from nurturing and from learning from other people.

In his book *In The Mind's Eye*,[4] Thomas G. West discusses visual thinkers and gifted people, many of whom have great talent but who also have learning difficulties, such as dyslexia or a poor memory. West argues that the possession of visual and spatial talents (as distinct from verbal or linguistic abilities) is indispensable, not only in the plastic arts, but also for the highest levels of original work in certain areas of science, engineering, medicine and mathematics. West's observations are of interest to this essay in that he draws a strong distinction between visual thinkers and wordsmiths.[5] West argues that to encourage talent and creativity, we should 'be more concerned with results than with trying to get everyone to learn things in the same way, especially if we are more interested in creating new knowledge than in merely absorbing and passing on old knowledge.'[6] West's argument corrects my thesis which, if taken too narrowly, might be taken to mean that craft should be taught (and learned) in the same way by everyone regardless of talent or character or need. The fact is that although bodies of knowledge are communal they are, of course, learned individually, consequently they need to be taught in a manner that recognizes this fact.

One virtue of learning with skilled practitioners, especially where they are also good teachers (which means that they are interested in the student, apprentice or pupil) is the greater possibility that exists for encouraging the individual pupil's own judgment and discrimination more or less from the beginning. Such good teaching practice came naturally to both Ann Hechle and Neal French.

Having talent makes a crucial difference to the quality of your work, and not having talent, or rather possessing some talent but not enough to make the first division, can be catastrophic: you give up. But giving up then denies you participation in something that gives your life meaning. The individual has then to weigh the advantages of being a player against the disadvantages of the disappointment of never becoming a star. This disappointment is mitigated for most of us because even though we are not excellent the presence of excellence in our chosen field gives it and us an enhanced value.

In broad terms I hope I describe how a beginner can, with the accomplishment of some of the rules of a craft, start to find a degree of independence in that craft. Independence is provided by the growing freedom of choice that comes with being able to do a range of new things and the greater refinement of judgment.

But being a beginner and being an expert are not the same thing. It was stated in Chapter One, pp. 22-3, and it has been implicit throughout Chapter Three, that expertise is open-ended: to be an expert is to have real creative power in the discovering of new goals and their attainment. In the previous chapter the emphasis was on the acquisition of the rules of a craft. The subject of this chapter is expertise and its relationship to the rules that organize it. Hence the question: do experts follow rules?

It is a philosopher, Ludwig Wittgenstein, who, in his explorations of what we know and how we know, offers a basis for understanding the general nature of craft knowledge. All craft activity is organized activity: it follows rules, conventions and patterns. The goal of a craft is not the practice of rules for their own sake but the successful accomplishment of a task – ideally, new, surprising and wonderful tasks. The difficulty is to establish just what the organizing role of rules is and Wittgenstein's insights can help us do this.

In Chapter Three I introduced the notion of 'constitutive' rules (see p. 42). As Allan Janik and others have argued this notion is very helpful in understanding the sort of knowledge that we call craft knowledge.[7]

The 'constitutive rules' that govern a particular kind of craft activity are not external to it: they are that craft activity. The rules that enable us to draw or paint or ride a bike are not separable from the activity. Rules, in the sense now under discussion, are the components of an activity which together add up to a body of knowledge. They cannot be divorced from that activity: if they are then you destroy that activity. To paint a portrait (a coloured likeness of a living model) is to obey the rules of portrait painting – not in the sense of obeying an order from someone else, but obeying the internal logic of an activity. It may help to view an activity, such as portrait painting, as a technology – it has physical 'laws' connected with the nature of light and pigments that will not go away just because you wish they were otherwise or because you do not like them. Or to take another example: to swim in the water you must move your arms or your legs or both in any one of a half dozen or more ways. In that sense you are obeying the internal logic of the activity.

The argument that will be developed from this is the one that you would expect from the tenor of the essay so far: knowledge gives you freedom of choice. However, it must be acknowledged that the acquisition of rules – the incorporation of rules into the fabric of the body and the texture of the mind – can cause the creative artist difficulties. For example, one of the warnings that Ann gave me early on in my learning how to draw letters was that if I got into the habit of holding the pen and nib at the wrong angle in relation to the page then I would find it very difficult to 'unlearn' my bad habit. For although it is the case that practical know-how gives you freedom of choice it is also the case that what is learned early on can trap you into bad habits.

Equally, whatever you go on to do as an independent practitioner, it is likely that you will carry with you at least something of the style of the tradition you were first taught. One of the consequences of craft knowledge being local knowledge – passed on from person to person and acquired through imitation as well as self-conscious analysis – is that you absorb a style. More anonymous vehicles of learning such as books, postal correspondence courses, or educational films and videos, although not bereft of style, are more distant, more sanitized and less personal in their influence. They are organized for a general audience, for whom it is felt necessary to order that information, tidy it up and subtract subjective elements. In the workshop or studio, however, the style of the flesh-and-blood teacher passes to the pupil (it is imitated by the pupil) and may never be completely removed. This is probably inevitable. Ridding yourself of your teacher can be difficult as you search for your own voice.

The fact is that the rules that govern or organize practical knowledge are not like clothes that you can put on or take off as the mood takes you. Unlike clothes, many of the rules of craft are neither easily won nor, once acquired, easily discarded. Yet without them one is practically naked.

In his *Philosophical Investigations*, Wittgenstein explores just the kind of rules that constitute craft activity.[8] Wittgenstein's prime concern is with language. In paragraph 199 Wittgenstein wrote: 'To understand a sentence means to understand a language. To understand a language means to be a master of a technique.'[9]

One of the observable characteristics about learning language or using it is that we do not consciously set out to learn by being taught rules, at least not explicitly. A young child does not learn to speak and understand what Mother or Father is saying by learning the explicit rules of grammar; these explicit rules demand an understanding of language in the first place. The child learns from people speaking to him and picks up the rules of speech without being aware that they are rules. I believe that Wittgenstein means that rules are embedded in and are inferred from practices – from events and experiences, from living – and not the other way around. The use of the word 'understand' is, however, equivocal. Most people are masters or mistresses of language in the sense that they make themselves understood and can understand others; they make judgments and puns and crack jokes.

They need not, however, be explicitly aware of the 'rules' of grammar. They use nouns, adjectives and verbs but need not know the rules 'governing' their use or, indeed, that the words they are using are nouns, adjectives and verbs.

As in language, then, so too in craft-based activities – including the ones outlined in the previous chapter – the theory of the activity does not describe the essence of the practice of that activity. The essence is in the activity itself but that activity is not random, it has its inner coherence which is understood by doing and becoming expert in that activity.

The relationship of theory to practice is complex and the subtleties will differ from practice to practice; but not to theorize is certainly not to claim that theory is unimportant. On the contrary, speculating about general principles that may apply to local practices can lead in the end to laws of nature and speculating about the elements of practice can bring about improvements in that practice. Think of any kind of coaching – be it in music, sport, dance or any kind of performance activity: it is the coach who, by reflecting upon aspects of a performance, helps both expert and beginner to improve.

The Norwegian philosopher, Kjell S. Johannessen, in a technical paper called 'Rule-Following and Intransitive Understanding',[10] explains that in Wittgenstein's argument there is an opposition between the interpretation and the application of a rule. There is a difference between knowing what a rule says and knowing how to apply it.

Arguably, however, one of the mistakes that beginners make in practice – as distinct from Wittgenstein's theory – is to begin by trying to interpret the rule. You think about it. You are prickling all over with self-awareness and puzzlement before committing brush to canvas or bow to string.

An American academic, Hubert L. Dreyfus, published a paper called 'Is Socrates to Blame for Cognitivism?'[11] Socrates is credited with the view that an expert is a person who can state the rules from which he or she proceeds. Dreyfus says that experts do not reason from rules. Rules, he says, if they are for anyone, are for beginners, not experts. He lists the stages we have to pass through:

a) Novice
b) Advanced beginner
c) Competence
d) Proficiency
e) Expertise

In explaining these stages, Dreyfus selects two examples: one is a bodily skill – driving a car; and the other is a mental skill – playing chess.

In chess the novice has to struggle to remember the rules governing the moving of the pieces on the board. The more advanced beginner, however, knows the moves and already recognizes some of the dangers on the board – such as getting caught in over-extended positions. At this stage there is, says Dreyfus, 'information overload'. One is aware of so much to attend to that it seems impossible to attend to all of it.

The next stage up from 'advanced beginner' is competence. The person who is competent can cope with a lot of information and will often manage to get things right but can also make serious mistakes. Dreyfus notes, apropos becoming a competent player at chess, that you make plans in your head and when these are successful you feel euphoria, when they fail 'you feel it in the pit of your stomach'.[12] You have achieved a competence in chess analysis but not a thorough control – you are still nervously aware of your propensity to make mistakes. And this nervousness, although Dreyfus does not say this, can subvert your competence.

Experts are not expected to be nervous (there is a difference between being nervous before one begins a project – acting, lecturing, starting an operation – and being nervous whilst one is actually doing it). Experts are expected to know what they are doing in the sense of being certain. (Certainty does not mean always being right.) Dreyfus remarks, 'Excellent chess players can play at the rate of 5-10 seconds a move ... at this speed they must depend almost entirely on intuition and hardly at all on analysis and comparison of alternatives.'[13]

Dreyfus argues that, in having any kind of expertise, one relies almost wholly on intuitions and not analysis. One does not 'think things through', one does them with certainty. Consequently, Dreyfus argues, experts do not use rules:

'If one asks an expert for strict rules one is forcing him back to the level of a beginner and asking him to state the rules he remembers but no longer uses when he has stored his experience of the actual outcomes of tens of thousands of situations.'[14] And he concludes that

> no amount of rules and facts can capture the knowledge that an expert has when he has stored his experience of the actual outcomes of tens of thousands of situations. The Socratic slogan 'If you can't explain it, you don't

> understand it' should be reversed: anyone who thinks he can carefully explain his skill, does not have expert understanding.[15]

Dreyfus's use of the word intuition is unfortunate, especially if we recall how appeals to intuition can be misused (as in the earlier illustration from David Hare's play *Murmuring Judges*). But we would be repeating Socrates' error if we concluded that because we cannot state what we know therefore we do not know anything. We demonstrate what we know through our actions. And, as I was at pains to stress in Chapter One, with the help of Polanyi (see p. 11), the sceptic must never drop his or her guard: claims to tacit knowledge, including and especially the expert's, can be subject to destructive analysis, to peer review, to criteria of success and failure.

In a way tacit knowledge contains within it the germ or the test of a severe morality. It is not what we say about skills that matters because what we say will always be incomplete – or even mendacious. What counts is what we do. The moral principle within craft is that each action shows that we are what we know. Each action might also show how much we care and what we care about. And although the nineteenth century's philosophy of the arts and crafts movement cannot be applied uncritically or without considerable adjustment to modern technological culture, nonetheless the attractiveness of such a philosophy is more than mere nostalgia, it is a recognition of how its fundamental precepts such as honesty and integrity in work as well as 'truth to materials' are expressions of the morality of practice.

Dreyfus's conclusion confirms Wittgenstein's argument that in following a rule the rule itself becomes the least important part of the activity. It is the doing of a rule, not its interpretation, that matters.

I am labouring this argument for two reasons. First, because Wittgenstein's and Dreyfus's thinking supports the thesis that 'real' knowledge includes tacit knowledge and that practice often precedes theory and that theory is embedded in and inferred from practice. Secondly, if rule-following is fundamentally about doing and not interpreting or conceptualizing, then it has consequences for contemporary prejudices in the plastic arts: that one can acquire a skill as and when the need for that skill arises.

If interpreting a rule and the rule itself are not the most important part of rule-following behaviour then the comforting thought that one can acquire a skill – such as drawing or carving – by reading a book, watching a video or some other interpretative form – is ill-founded. Practical knowledge is not just there for the taking, it is not for taking down from the shelf, and it is not like book learning.

It is that very aspect of craft knowledge that appears to be a matter of extreme irritation to some intellectuals, especially to those who feel that they themselves would like to participate in a craft. The expertise that Dreyfus describes expresses itself in spontaneity. That spontaneity, that fluency which is the goal of the artist, is an extraordinary sight. It is something that those of us who are not artists or performers or experts admire and envy. And what we envy is the certainty and the freedom that certainty generates.

This spontaneity is, however, informed – it is knowledgeable, it is the product of practice, of rote learning, and – as important – of the ever increasing finesse of one's judgments. For most people such freedom to create as is contained in the knowledge of informed spontaneity is not lightly earned; but it is a characteristic of the twentieth century that intellectuals believe they can sidestep the work and go directly to a level of spontaneity without the necessity of practice or Dreyfus's 'tens of thousands of experiences'. The first move in the intellectual's stripping out of the craft from art in order to appropriate art for themselves is, of course, to downgrade the craft element (see Chapter Two). The second step is to uncouple 'creativity' from 'craft'.

There are generally three stages in the intellectuals' sleight of hand when it comes to craft issues. The first is to begin by trying to take the learning of the craft seriously. The second is the realization that learning the craft is going to require much more time (and humility) than first envisaged. The third stage, because their own efforts are, understandably, not very good, is to dismiss the craft element as 'sterile and rule-bound' and claim as more expressive their 'freer' efforts. An additional stage is then to publish a book, the function of which is to provide wordy meanings of their art work and also to provide a theoretical basis for their rejection of the craft.

A classic example of the intellectual's sleight of hand regarding craft knowledge is provided by a psychoanalyst called Marion Milner who spent many years 'learning' to paint. This resulted in her writing a book, *On Not Being Able to Paint*, first published in 1950 and reprinted many times since.[16]

Milner begins by saying she is not satisfied with her progress as an artist and that what she has produced feels counterfeit to her.[17] She says she would find herself inspired by an object or a scene and so would try to draw. However, the results of her efforts generally disappointed her. She claimed that 'no doubt' the drawing was a fairly accurate copy of an object but it produced 'despairing boredom'.[18] And throughout the book, whenever she faces herself with the task of setting down a 'realistic' representation of what is in front of her, she calls the results of what she does 'counterfeit' or 'dry' or 'lifeless'. Unfortunately she provides no illustrations of this work which she is so sure to call 'fairly accurate'.

She decides that the problem with her drawing is that it is inexpressive. She discovered a 'determination to try to state pictorially something of the inner brooding quality of nature rather than her accidental appearances' and consequently she developed a means of free drawing which she describes like this:

> This is to draw a little, at random, spots, shadings or lines, then feel what these suggest and let the line go on, holding both it and the idea it suggests in mind, as it were organically with a whole body awareness, not trying to develop thought line by line but letting the hand go where it will and letting the line call forth an answer from the thought.[19]

In other words, you have an idea to start you off, but give it up as soon as the lines you draw suggest something else. This is a much easier task than drawing from memory or from life.

In the research that follows, she continues with the free drawing, but remains uninterested and wholly bored by 'conventional' drawing, although she implies that conventional drawing is somehow less demanding for her, describing it as a refuge:

> I often want to take refuge in the 'trying to draw something' method, in which one thinks of something, for instance a donkey, and tries to make the lines go right, not letting them have their say at all and allowing no interplay ... This I find produces an infinitely dull drawing.[20]

As a psychoanalyst, Milner describes her own drawings not in terms of aesthetics, composition or observation, but in terms of myths and emotions. She provides elaborate literary interpretations of her 'simple' drawings which she builds onto the scantily drawn images. Here are some of her remarks about a free drawing which she called 'The Mount of Olives': 'the bones sticking up out of the sand make me think of "The Skeleton under the Sea", the blasted olive tree on the left is a little like the blasted beeches, and also brings to mind the storm in *King Lear*.'[21]

Yet such is the unspecific nature of the drawing, it could be used to recall all manner of other associations. As a drawing it is rather like a coat peg – you hang what you like from it. Milner seems to remain unaware, as do hundreds of artists these days, of the distinction between an object – sculpture, painting or drawing – being said to represent an idea as opposed to expressing it. You can make virtually any object 'represent' whatever you like. You just say 'Let this represent that'. But this is not the same as claiming that 'This thing expresses that' (see Chapter Two, pp. 34-5).

Milner replaces drawing and painting with words. For although she goes on to present a number of free drawings in which various figures and scenes occur these do not appear to have much quality either as images or as drawings (although it is hard to tell quality of line from relatively poor reproductions). What matters are the explanations she provides for these drawings. Milner is a knowledgeable, skilled analyst and she compensates for the deficiencies of her craft of drawing and painting by her abilities in analysis and literature.

She wants to create art that is rich but wants to do it without the craft. For example, there is a passage where she describes a scene depicting a harbour, the sea and a developing storm. She would like to paint it and her words capture the painterly challenge very well: 'There was green water darkening towards the horizon and looming sky much darker than the sea. In the foreground, waves glistening white against the green, white sand close in shore, some terns, whiter than all against the darkening sea.'[22]

Such is the vividness of the description that one can imagine how one might itch to get this scene down on paper in a manner that captures its drama. The drama, it will be noticed, exists in part in the movement of sky and water, but also and especially in the heightened contrasts of tone and colour. There will be other aspects that the artist can only hope the picture would suggest, such as the smell of the air and sea, and the sound of the wind and water and the cries of sea birds. But to make any progress with a visual interpretation of this scene (rather than any other imagery that it happens to prompt in your mind) there are a number of technical, practical problems to be solved.

Consider what Jan Gordon has to say about painting out of doors in his *A Stepladder to Painting.* One of the problems that strikes the painter, especially the amateur, is the discrepancy between the brilliance of the sky, sunshine and highlights, and the limited powers of white paint. In Milner's case the sky is looming but she has a problem with three different levels of white – glistening white water, white sand and white sea birds. Is each the same or different in tone from one another? Everyday outdoor light can can be both much brighter (and its shadows darker) than 'anything mere paint can reach'[23] and if the three whites are each different from one another then how do you cope? One way, if you have mastered the craft of recognizing tone values, and have memorized a palette that allows you to match or interpret tone values is to make your painting a tone or more generally darker than the scene you are painting. This means that whilst the tones within the painting are in the same kind of relationship that you see in the external scene, each is darker than its real equivalent. Another way is to distribute the loss of one or two tones throughout the painting so that each tone is marginally weaker than it is in nature. Both approaches offer the means of dealing with the problems that confront the painter and may be viewed as genuinely liberating.

The fact is that Milner failed to 'go native' in the body of knowledge she was ostensibly interested in – indeed, she fled from the difficulties of it because she was put off, for understandable reasons, by the sheer slog and disappointment that the amateur or beginner almost inevitably endures in the first months or even years of study.

Craft knowledge is genuine knowledge. To possess it in any form is to see the world in an enriched way compared with someone who does not possess it. There is nothing magical about this. If you are a dentist, for example, you cannot help noticing the shape of people's mouths and cheeks and making inferences about the state and number of their teeth. A dentist interested in Rembrandt and Rembrandt's followers has a field day studying the dental condition of the seventeenth-century Dutch citizen. One reason why some portraits of the period look sad is probably because both painter and subject had toothache.

Or take another example: having done a little lettering I can spot crass examples of bad signage – poorly spaced letters or words, inappropriate use of upper-case letters and so forth. But professional letterers, people whose eyes are genuinely knowledgeable, sometimes despair of communicating their criticisms to the rest of the world, especially to the authorities who commission and accept the signs in the first place. The professionals' problems are compounded by the fact that those officials with whom they are dealing cannot see the problem: they do not have the knowledge.

The more general question is: how does one convince those people who are writers or wordsmiths of one kind or another of the radical difference between craft knowledge and propositional knowledge? Craft knowledge keeps getting drowned out by those who want either to relegate it to knowledge that is 'mechanical and separate from imagination' or who seem to insist that anything done in the plastic arts can be translated into words. Or who, like Milner, keep reinstating the hierarchy of making what ever is said about an object more important than the object itself. Milner's principle mistake is that she refuses to see the difference between painting and writing about painting.

5 Form and Content

In its most interesting and creative form, the practice of practical knowledge is an open-ended activity. It is to be contrasted with the concept of skill acquisition as a 'skill loop', whereby you learn enough to achieve a goal and no more. By this I am thinking of people who acquire and practise tricks such as writing the Lord's Prayer on the back of a postage stamp. Other examples are people who acquire skills with the intent of securing a straightforward commercial profit: for example, the production of paintings for turning into Christmas or birthday cards. The production of painting or sculpture or craft to suit picturesque or sentimental conventions tends to be built around a series of closed formulas.

Formula art resembles the condition of design and manufacture of a product, whereby having fixed the nature of the design through prototypes, you then produce the object in quantity without further development. It is not only picturesque art or populist craft that is formulaic, however. There is so-called avant-garde art and craft which is equally conventional in its own terms and whose design and content has been shaped by a market, albeit one that is different from the market for picturesque art and craft.

However, craft processes need not be reduced to formulas. In this chapter I wish to look at the reciprocity that exists between the exercise of craft skill and the subject matter that is articulated through it.

Subject matter is often a problem for the contemporary plastic artist and for the individual artist the question 'What should I be making in art?' is a continuous anxiety. And yet it appears that many people have been drawn into making art who like the idea of being an artist but lack a subject. Unsurprisingly in such circumstances there is more anxiety about the 'why' of art than the 'how'.

In 1927, R. H. Wilenski, an art critic and art historian, published a book called *The Modern Movement in Art.*[1] It is a clear-sighted explanation and defence of the modern movement. He argued that for the last five hundred years in Western art, since religion ceased to be the focus of the artist's work, all intelligent artists have been tormented by a search for a justification for their work. The fundamental problem since the High Renaissance has been finding a justification 'for artistic work and a criterion of its value other than the justification and criterion afforded by the service of some religion'.[2]

An interesting history of Western art could be written tracking the politics of each rise and fall of the many theories and movements which have been hailed as the 'real' justification or purpose for making art. Two contrasting movements in the twentieth century are a) art as a celebration of the people (Social Realism) and b) Color-field painting, derived from the art critic Clement Greenberg's insistence that the painter should concentrate on painting itself – flat colour and the quality of the pigments. With the benefit of hindsight we can see that the effort that went into these justifications, policing them, trying to get everyone to participate in them, was doomed to failure in the long term (in the short term the effort proved quite fruitful). Greenberg, for example, argued that flatness was the proper subject for painting: 'Whereas one tends to see what is in an Old Master before seeing it as a picture, one sees a Modernist painting as a picture first. This is, of course, the best way of seeing any kind of picture, Old Master or Modernist, but Modernism imposes it as the only and necessary way, and Modernism's success in doing so is a success of self-criticism.'[3] But at the same time even Greenbergian dogma was productive. Some of the paintings that it encouraged have given delight and may be valued by future generations for their intrinsic worth.

Reviewing Western art in the twentieth century we might acknowledge two lessons. First, the justifications for making art are more ephemeral than the best of the art itself. Secondly, the value of a justification – be it nature, metaphysics, social realism, feminist critiques, Greenbergian modernism, or a belief in Freud or Jung – lies not in its truth but in its coherence. A framework of values is provided within which the artist can construct her or his work. I would think, however, although I have no proof, that as an artist, in order for a theory or movement to be useful to you, you have to believe in it. I cannot imagine how you would produce good art if you were sceptical about the framework within which you were working. Your scepticism would make your enterprise seem pointless and unless you were impelled by some other motive – the need to earn a living or get a degree – then there would be no point in going on with the work.

The movements and 'isms' in art since 1945 have tended to be the products of either fashion or desperation. Many do not offer a coherent structure of values; and some are so contrived as to be apart from the notion of value altogether.

Consider, for instance, the short-lived international art movement of the 1980s called Neo-Geo. This was the name given to a revival of non-expressionistic abstract painting in the mid-1980s ('Neo' for revival; 'Geo' for geometric). Its arbitrariness and desperation is well caught – albeit unintentionally – by Anna Moszynska in her book *Abstract Art*:

> 'Neo-Geo' as it is known (amongst other things), was a self-conscious style, aware of its own manipulations and 'appropriations' of extant forms of art – hence 'neo' in the sense of revival and imitation, rather than 'new'. Unlike its figurative predecessor [European Figuration of the early 1980s], however, Neo-Geo was the child of Pop, Minimal and Conceptual art as well as of technology and critical (sociological and structural) discourse. Rather than appealing to the senses or the emotions, it was cooler, more distanced, critical of, yet curiously complicit with, the consumer society that helped it to shoot to fame. Encompassing a great many disparate artists, Neo-Geo did not form a cohesive group, although it became a convenient marketing label.[4]

In the crafts there has been a strong tradition of usefulness and utilitarian demand for handicraft wares until the twentieth century. This usefulness took various forms ranging from functional utility, such as things for the kitchen or the workplace, to commercial, domestic and institutional decoration. You could commission decoration for your church or town hall or your home. The production of useful decoration continues: in designing textiles, wallpapers, plaster mouldings, building materials and tableware, the contemporary applied artist will take his or her cue from popular sentiment and the market place. Not so the contemporary studio craftsperson.

The modern studio craftsperson has altered the relationship between handicraft and usefulness. In the early years of the twentieth century educated middle-class men and women began interesting themselves in the handicraft of former trade activities such as pottery or dyeing and weaving. They did so in order to build a life around the routines of practical work as well as to make beautiful objects. But they did not want these routines to become too punishing. The pain of commercial craft was transformed by turning trade craft into art craft.

Once the notion developed among purchasers as well as studio craftspeople that studio craft was a form of art, then the art aspect quickly came to dominate. Studio craftspeople still make functional objects, but increasingly 'function' is the subject matter and not the purpose; the purpose is art. Consider lettering, whose utilitarian form we see every day of our lives. Most is not done by hand, although a surprising amount of the lettering we see has handicraft roots. We also see it in a more decorative context: as the special signage for grand public buildings or for uplifting inscriptions in such places as churches or museums.

Over the last forty years there has been disagreement about the art, the craft and the design of lettering. One of the assumptions made by some artist-letterers has been that in order to increase the 'art' or the 'feeling' or the 'expressive' content in lettering, one must suppress or eliminate the functional aspects. This reduces or increases (depending upon your point of view) the status of lettering to abstract drawing. The scholar and art historian Nicolete Gray, a heroine of the artist-letterers, has written with great knowledge and sensitivity about lettering as an art in her book *Lettering as Drawing*.[5] It is an inspirational book in which Gray argues that abstract art has liberated all artists, including letterers, to be as figurative or literal as they wish or need to be. Gray says students should be skilled, but she makes a distinction between skill and knowledge.[6] This contentious distinction is partly a product of the time at which the book was written (1970) – a period when liberal opinion in the arts was especially hostile towards the concept of skill. Gray wrote, 'This book therefore aims to teach not skill but knowledge; the modern artist has his own, new, very various and expanding skills.'[7] A more recent version of this argument was put by Anna Moszynka in *Abstract Art* (see Chapter Two, p. 29). Both Gray and Moszynka are wrong in seeing a variety of individually held and fragmented techniques as proof of an expansion of skill (see Chapter Two, pp. 34-9). Moreover, it is a central argument of this essay that skill is knowledge.

A significant thesis in Gray's book is that lettering cannot reach its potential as an art if it is taught 'classically' (such as in the manner of Edward Johnston, a man whom she praises but whose teachings she considers out of date and irrelevant to the present day).[8] Moreover, lettering, in her view, has to transcend utility.

The evidence she gives for denying the usefulness of 'classical' skills is negligible but her case for liberalizing the content of lettering is strong: she cites examples of lettering used as pure art as long ago as the twelfth century. Yet the examples she chooses to praise from this century have been produced by people whose knowledge resides in their skill, such as Paul Klee, Rudolf Koch and Imre Reiner. This knowledge gives them a freedom to break rules. Not only that, their skill knowledge enables them to make the breaking of rules the subject matter of their work. The content of the work of the first and second generation of twentieth-century modernists was the replacing of conventions, rules, meaning and utility with novelty. Today's artist-letterers are not so fortunate because the option – the final option – of questioning the tradition of the craft has been used up.

However, 'writing' without meaning becomes an arid exercise after a time. Consequently artist-letterers have not stopped writing, drawing or carving useful words or texts although they frequently paint, write, draw, carve, engrave or sandblast alphabets in various degrees of clarity and expression as a halfway house between functional work and abstraction. Some letterers, wanting the freedom to be themselves, still wish to bring words or sentences back into their work; they have turned to the production of aphorisms as their excuse for making art. Mostly these are sayings taken from existing works of literature, theology or philosophy.

Aphorisms can be tolerable when they have an appropriate context – such as a church or civic building, a school or a university. But out of context, hand-crafted aphorisms sold as free-standing or wall-mounted art objects for the home come close to being kitsch. An exhibition in 1993 in London by internationally famous artist-letterers contained many examples of the genre, such as: 'Pride, the Never-Failing Vice of Fools'; 'My Eyes Eavesdrop on their Lashes'; 'I am Finished with the Ordinary! What Use has Halter, Bridle to One who has Shaken off Contrivance?'

More generally, we have seen that for fine artists and studio craftspeople alike, the natural tendency, in the absence of any outside subject matter or purpose, has been to make art about themselves. Sometimes this self-reflexive art has taken the form of abstract or figurative expressionism in which the intention is to leave a deeply personal mark for the world to see. Such work is produced in the belief that every piece of art is a unique expression of a unique individual.

It may be trivially true that every piece of art says something about the artist, but the weight of this 'truth' can be debated. After all, we have only to consider how many paintings once attributed to Rembrandt are no longer attributed to Rembrandt to be puzzled by what we really mean by the 'unique signature' of the artist. In any event, after a while, 'uniqueness' ceases to be an interesting quality.

The pursuit of self-expression has meant that it has become increasingly difficult to distinguish between art and art therapy. It has become apparent that many men and women see making art as some kind of curative activity for themselves whilst, at the same time, hoping it will interest a public.

Art as therapy is self-obsessed and made without reference by the 'artist' to how it will be taken or understood by other people. Art which is not therapy is generally understood as being for an audience whose interests are not exclusively pathological as is the case with patients, their art therapists, and their doctors. The art critic Flint Schier puts matters well in this respect when he suggests, 'The artist must imagine the community he or she is painting for and wonder how the work will strike that community.'[9]

Yet some art educationalists appear unconcerned at the blurring of art with therapy and have argued that the point of art is to express yourself to yourself. Take, for example, a book called *No More Secondhand Art: Awakening the Artist Within* by Peter London, Professor of Art History and an art therapist.[10]

His book encourages everyone to be an artist. Because most people think that art – painting, sculpting, pottery and carving – is beyond them, Professor London goes to great lengths to remove hurdles to their self-confidence. London's desire to point out that most of us are capable of making pots or paintings to some sort of standard is both reasonable and laudable. The youngsters who worked in the Florentine workshops of the Italian Renaissance producing paintings and sculptures under the direction of their masters were not geniuses: and, like them, most of us could learn to draw, model or paint just as most of us learn to read, write and do arithmetic.[11] London is right to say that the largest hurdle for most of us to overcome in art is our belief that making art is the sole province of genius or, at any rate, special talent. The best art, like the best of anything, is probably the preserve of special people, but if only the best were permissible then a great many of us, whatever our profession, would be kicking our heels.

London, however, removes the fear of inadequacy by a sleight of hand. He coins a concept called 'non-competitive knowing'. He explains that when he was a child he got depressed because he was seldom first in class and there were always other people brighter or more talented than he. Then he says he realized that there was one subject upon which he alone was the supreme expert – himself.[12]

London goes on: 'This non-competitive knowing is a special reward of creative enterprises. It is quite delicious to carry out an investigation, personally arrive at a response, and not feel compelled to measure the worth of your findings against those of others.'[13]

London has removed two obstacles in the path of the would-be artist. He has removed any difficulty about how to do art, and he has removed the difficulty of why to do it. You do not have to worry about technical incompetence because you are no longer comparing your work with anyone else's and your subject matter is yourself.

Objectively this is a recipe for the destruction of the plastic arts. It suggests an autistic approach to knowledge coupled with an obsession with the inner self; an inner self that is likely to be ignorant since the direct implication of London's thesis is that you need not bother to learn from others. It is a further refinement of the process of fragmentation of the knowledge that underpins the plastic arts in their traditional forms (see Chapter Two p. 36), in which you invent a technique to call your own and pursue it without reference to the wider craft or body of knowledge of your art. This fragmentation, coupled to a naïve view of the expression of self, will just about finish off the plastic arts for good.

Arguably, if you stay within the boundaries of 'non-competitive knowing' it would appear that the initial freedoms become constraints. For if you stay within the confines of non-competitive knowing, producing objects that only you know how to assess, then it is possible, indeed probable, that you will be limiting yourself to an aesthetic which is private or, as I suggest, autistic.

Human knowledge is created communally. If you decide not to compare your work or your ideas with those of other people then you withdraw from the culture of discoveries, inventions, innovations, techniques and insights. You give yourself the awesome task of having to discover everything on your own.

Yet it should be conceded that sometimes, if the individual really possesses something of substance out of which he or she wants to make art, then it is possible for that individual to 'guess it all' or at least 'guess enough'. Much depends on what impels the person towards expression in art. It is one thing for Peter London to subtitle his book *Awakening the Artist Within,* but it does seem to matter that the artist within has a subject worth articulating. And on this point I wish to look at the case of the English painter Alfred Wallis.

Alfred Wallis (1855-1942) is described as a primitive.[14] His paintings are simple and apparently childlike. He painted pictures of boats, seas, skies, cliffs, quaysides, houses and fish with directness. There is no fine detail. The colours are generally subdued – it is a 'marine' palette: 'Black, green, white and ochre, occasionally introducing pink or blue, were practically all the colours he used, and he seldom used more than three of these at once.'[15] Most of the works are on cardboard and the paints he used were the same as those used for painting real boats.

Wallis worked for many years as a merchant seaman, on schooners and then steamers that sailed the Atlantic between Cornwall and Newfoundland. He gave up deep-sea sailing for local fishing. He was semi-literate, obsessed with the Bible, reclusive and, in the end, probably mad. He started painting when he was seventy shortly after he was widowed.

I infer from *Alfred Wallis: Primitive*, the biography by Sven Berlin (who knew him), that Wallis wanted some constructive way of occupying his time. It is unlikely that Wallis regarded painting as therapeutic, in the sense of being in some way a cure for his madness, not least because it is unlikely that he saw himself as mad. In any case the works themselves are not images made by a man painting his demons. Wallis painted charming pictures of ships. Nonetheless there is a case for arguing that his paintings were his autobiography.

Wallis was discovered in 1928 by two professional artists: Ben Nicholson and Christopher Wood. Dennis Farr, author of *English Art 1870-1940*, says of paintings by Nicholson between 1928 and 1930 that they 'have a quality of childlike enchantment and arbitrariness of scale that helps to explain why Nicholson ... should have greeted the work of Alfred Wallis with such sympathetic enthusiasm.'[16]

The discovery of an artist, especially one as idiosyncratic as Wallis, is an interesting phenomenon in itself. Today there are hundreds of thousands of fans of Wallis worldwide but I wonder how many of us would have seen the quality in Wallis's work if it had not been taken from obscurity and placed in galleries and books? I doubt if I would have recognized his quality unaided if I had come across his work, unknown and unregarded in a junk shop.

But are there other factors that led to Wallis being discovered? Was Wallis an unskilled but expressive amateur? What was Wallis expressing? And were the deficiencies in his craft of painting compensated by craft knowledge of a different kind?

Nicholson was a participant in the 'modern movement'. Wallis's directness, his economy of drawing and painting (in his work the two things are often synonymous), and his austere palette would have coincided with Nicholson and Wood's emerging modernist interests.

It is salutary, however, to remind ourselves how art language encourages or represses our sympathies. For another way of describing Wallis's work, a way which holds true for the many bad paintings he produced, need not be couched in the positive terms of 'directness', 'economy of line' or 'austere palette' but in terms of lack of finesse, inability to construct perspectives and ignorance of colour.

Berlin argues that Wallis was a stern realist who struggled exceptionally hard to try and make his paintings right. And his standards of 'rightness' were high because he painted what he knew. As a seaman Wallis was also an artisan and artisans are often literal, they deal in concrete facts. Of Wallis, Berlin notes, 'It was nearly always his practice to paint the sea grey or white, pointing out that if you took a glass of seawater and held it up to the light, it was not green or purple or blue but colourless.'[17]

Berlin notes, 'in his conscious mind he was trying to paint life as he saw it, naturalistically – or rather, realistically … and it was with real problems he struggled.'[18]

In Chapter Four I discussed another amateur painter, Marion Milner (pp. 65-7). The contrast between Milner's intellectually sophistical ways of avoiding the struggle to set down pictures and Wallis's determination to see the struggle through could not be greater or more ironic. Ironic because Milner wrote at length about trying to set up a dialogue with her 'subconscious', whilst Wallis was convinced the devil was sending voices to him via radio transmissions sent down his chimney and – I conjecture – was more likely trying to shut out the cacophony of his 'voices' out of his art.

Wallis did not have words, as Milner had words, to talk himself out of his difficulties with his painting. He had to persist with a craft that would give him what he was after, the articulation of his lifetime's craft – the sea. His expertise as a mariner and a fisherman gives his work a coherence and his inabilities with language meant he could only act according to the rule that painting is not writing, practice is not theorizing. It was Wallis who said, 'I guessed it all'.[19] But he also did it on the foundation of a lifetime's practical experience; it was knowledge not easily won.

I have taken Wallis as an example for the following reasons. His lack of craft knowledge in the sphere of painting can be taken as a rebuttal of the need for painters to acquire complex craft knowledge. But I am suggesting that he had considerable craft knowledge, and that his practical understanding in one sphere of craft compensated for his lack of understanding in another: his subject matter carries him through. His art is distinguished by certain characteristics which are rooted in his expertise as a seaman: there is an orderliness about the way many of his pictures are composed; there is an accuracy in the placing of sails, and masts and the proportions of these to the hulls of the ships; and a sense of pattern is demonstrated in the placing of the elements around the picture surface – a sense of pattern that might be developed in a man who has spent a lifetime working with the functional patterns of furled and unfurled sails, rope ladders, fishing nets and so forth. These elements give him his subject matter and they also contain some of the aesthetic elements we admire in his work. As was suggested earlier, subject matter is as great a gift to the artist as talent.

But I am also interested in the relationship here between intention and process. I am interested in what Wallis intended to do and how far he felt hampered by his inability to solve some of the problems he faced.

As a painter, Wallis fits with the Peter London 'non-competitive knowing' concept. (As a seaman he would have served an apprenticeship, learned from others and lived his craft communally.) Wallis lived and painted in St Ives in Cornwall. Since the early 1900s St Ives had been host to a large colony of artists attracted to the town by the light and the climate. But Wallis ignored all the artists in St Ives and in his turn he was ignored by all of them except Berlin, Nicholson and a very few others. These others did not attempt to teach him and he did not attempt to learn from them. In his madness and acute bloody-mindedness, he was, one might say, autistic.

Was he not frustrated by what he could not do and what he did not know? How often were his intentions as an artist thwarted by his lack of knowledge of process? After all, for most painters, sculptors and other studio craftspersons there is an interdependency between the content and the execution in a work of art or craft. But if your ability in process is curtailed, then surely so is your intention.

The relationship between intention and process is considered by Michael Baxandall, Professor of the History of Classical Tradition at London's Warburg Institute, in his book *Patterns of Intention*.[20] One of Baxandall's observations concerns the nature of problem solving. He describes a problem as being 'a state of affairs in which two things hold: something is to be done, and there is no purely habitual or simply reactive way of doing it.'[21]

Now there are two aspects to how the problem can be solved. You may proceed austitically and attempt to guess it all. This is a high risk strategy for various reasons. First, you run a grave risk of failure: you may fail to realize your intention. Secondly, you may waste your time. As discussed in Chapter One (see p. 10), the usefulness of theory lies in its ability to leapfrog the slow task of having to work everything out empirically. A similar situation holds here. You have to decide whether it is worth trying to solve a problem on your own, and perhaps solve every problem on your own, or whether it is worth looking at what others have done in the past. The choice may be economic (in the sense of time) as much as moral or artistic.

One of Wallis's paintings, which is reproduced in Berlin's biography, shows two sailing ships circling a lighthouse. The view he has chosen to paint from is very difficult because we are looking down on the scene. In the event he shows one of the sailing ships on its side – it is, in 'real' terms, capsized.

The main elements of the painting, including the boat on its side, are elegantly composed but was Wallis happy? Did it look right to him – as a 'stern realist'? We may be beguiled by the charm of the childishness of Wallis' solution but is it less beguiling if we think that perhaps this was not what Wallis wanted, but he simply had no choice? In other words, Wallis had not intended to paint a ship on its side but had to because he had no knowledge of the process that would enable him to paint the ship with the bow pointing towards us and the bulk of the ship foreshortened.

If we consider the relationship between process and intention more generally it is, as Baxandall says, unlikely that in the making of a piece of art that the artist's intentions remain fixed from start to finish.

Baxandall observes that one of the reasons we value paintings – and I would add one-off handicraft items of many kinds, including ceramics and sculpture – is that they are not designed. That is to say that the process of making by hand allows the maker's intentions to develop and change in response to what he or she is creating over a period of time. Baxandall says,

> A static notion of intention, supposing just a preliminary stance to which the final product either more or less conforms, would deny a great deal of what makes pictures worth bothering about, whether for us or for their makers. It would deny the encounter with the medium and reduce the work to a sort of conceptual or ideal art imperfectly realized.[22]

Industrial design is a form of ideal art. The essence of the designer's work is to create a plan from which other people can make, usually in quantity, perfect objects which require no modification during construction and which do not require the designer to be on hand giving directions. In reality a design is usually the creation, not of one person, but of a team of designers and engineers. Many prototypes, trial runs and other creative tasks are completed before this ideal state of affairs is achieved, by which an intention is fixed throughout a production process.

By contrast, making one-off things by hand allows you to change your mind as the work is proceeding in front of you. This in turn is partly (and strongly) influenced by what you are capable of doing practically. There is a 'dialogue' between you and the object you are making, and the medium is your practical skill.

Certain kinds of studio craft, however, gain their attractiveness to us by virtue of a conflict. A production potter making teasets of matching cups and saucers, teapots and milk jugs is trying in fact to keep to a fixed intention. Unlike a painter or a ceramic sculptor, the production artist-potter is trying to keep his intentions static because he wants a uniformity of shape. Equally, however, it is the near impossibility of the handicraft process to duplicate forms exactly that gives the work its attractive, non-mechanical frisson. It is the tension between the inevitable vagaries of handicraft with the conscious desire of keeping to a static intention, a repeated design, that combines to make the handicraft production potter's work special.

Other studio crafts in which repetitive work is involved exhibit a similar productive tension between the accidental vagaries of the handicraft process and the desire to maintain a static intention.

Edward Johnston, writing about formal penmanship, is particularily interesting on this. He states that formal penmanship is primarily a useful handicraft and that its product is to be read. Consequently the writing should simply flow on like the letters of a printed book. Therefore the good scribe cultivates uniformity of action until it becomes habitual and is 'approaching the mechanical'. Yet Johnston insists on calling such writing 'free'.[23] For he says that the good scribe simultaneously cultivates an alertness 'ready to spring at a chance'.[24] How can this be? What room for chance is there given a) that one is disciplined to stay within the demands of the form of the alphabet and b) that one is subservient to the demands of readability and legibility?

There are what Johnston calls 'varieties'.[25] These may be small or large. They can be introduced only if they are to the mutual advantage of the manuscript or design you are creating and to the words of the author. They could be changes or breaks in the flow of the text that suddenly strike one as right as one proceeds (or which are foreseen as right at the planning stage). These varieties are to do with degrees of emphasis – of position, spacing, arrangement, form, size, weight and colour.

Johnston speaks of the scribe 'daring to introduce' varieties, but in truth his entire approach is towards encouraging the scribe to be an expert such that he or she knows when it is right to spring at a chance. As this essay has discussed earlier (see pp. 63-4), experts do not reflect about rules – they push forward with the certainty of rules acquired, reflected upon, embedded and 'forgotten'. Johnston does not talk about expertise, instead he introduces, as a metaphor, the idea of the scribe being like a stream, carefree, his pen racing with the text, mind flying: 'In an instant the pen leaps or twists, touching the straightforward flow with variety – from the common, less visible subtleties, to the rare, most striking significance.'[26]

A studio craftsperson such as a production artist-potter or an artist-scribe has some licence, as an artist as well as a craftsperson, to allow (small) variations of intention to evolve as the process of making develops. In one-off works, such as painting or sculpture, the licence to depart from the original intention is considerable – such licence being one of the points about making original paintings or sculptures. With regard to the process of painting and the evolution of intention, Baxandall begins with a remark made by Cézanne and taken up by Picasso: every brushstroke changes a picture. With each brushstroke the painter finds himself facing a new situation. 'For instance,' says Baxandall, 'the addition of a new tone or hue can modify the relationships and the phenomenal character of the previously placed tones and hues; and because of the simultaneous presence of the elements of a picture this effect is very powerful, however clearly the painter has in mind a final character.'[27]

Baxandall's description of painting rings true, but think how nonsensical it becomes if we imagined that the painter could not recognize how the relationships are changed. To see that they are changed is but one small act of discrimination, to understand how is a major one. It is this that accounts for the substantial difference between painting with and without serious intent.

We might also note that intentions not only develop in the process of making artefacts – be they paintings or pots – but they develop when the artist is not making her own work but thinking about and looking at other people's work. This is an active process. Again Baxandall has a point to make on this.[28] He asks us to reconsider our understanding of the notion of artistic influence. We tend to talk glibly of X being influenced by Y but in fact the powerful connection is the other way around. X finds something that interests him in Y's work. That is what happened with Ben Nicholson and Alfred Wallis. It is not that Wallis influenced Nicholson so much as Nicholson, turning over ideas in his own mind and in his own work, saw something in Wallis's work that made sense, something he could learn from and use.

It is another reason why Peter London's autistic approach to art is wrong-headed: most artists find, develop, evolve, and clarify their intentions through a wide-ranging 'dialogue' with what other people are doing. Often the dialogue is competitive: think, for example, of the fruitful but competitive friendship of Braque and Picasso.

The relationship between handicraft process and intentions can be intellectually complex especially when there are ambitions for achieving conceptual and emotional content as well as creating sensuous visual delight. And since Wallis produced slender art in respect of conceptual and emotional content, I want to turn to another, entirely different artist, the Dutch painter, Judith Leyster (1609-60).

I have chosen her painting *Two Children with a Kitten and an Eel* partly through pleasure but also because it is old enough to have survived the test of time and changing tastes.

Now, as Simon Schama says in his book *The Embarrassment of Riches*,[29] the painting catches the two children in a half mood between teasing and spitefulness. The boy is cheerful and clutches a kitten in one arm and holds an eel in his left hand; his younger sister looks equally gleeful but appears to be indicating that she thinks her brother is crazy. On one level this is a moralizing painting – or rather it would have been understood as such by the seventeenth-century Dutch audience. The kitten represents playfulness (and waywardness) and the eel represents slipperiness – of children, adults, events, and life. Therefore the painting can be read both in terms of truisms about the nature of children, and about the nature of adults (the child is the father – or mother – of the man).

But although the painting is aphoristic and moralizing it is not at all an example of the leaden smugness to be seen, for example, in the self-congratulatory art-craft work of the modern letterers discussed above. Conceptually,

Leyster's painting is sophisticated both in the knowledge that she discloses and in the expectations she has of the audience for her painting.

The commentary on children in general is a consequence of the way in which the suggestion of playful naughtiness and spite has been suggested in the children's expressions. The addition of the animals is conceptually astute. They make us reflect upon how children behave; we know that these creatures might later be handled kindly by the children or, just as easily, they might be tormented to death. In the painting of the children's faces there is care and Leyster, I believe, shows love but not sentimentality. The flesh she has painted suggests brutishness as much as innocence.

That Leyster had an idea of what she wanted to portray before she began is undeniable – her prior intention is shown by the symbolism in the painting and the careful posing of the models. Additionally, as Baxandall is at pains to stress, artists do not cut themselves off from the ideas of the time. The symbolism of such as innocence versus knowingness and domestic peace and public chaos was a common currency in the visual and literary arts of the period. Yet the original intention would in all probability have evolved and deepened as Leyster progressed.

What Leyster achieves is both an approximation of a moment in time and a complex commentary on the nature of children. The painting looks like a moment caught in time but it is really an idea about a moment in time, a suggestion of what a moment in time looks like. This is not a photograph. The kitten jumped from the boy's arms and the eel died long before the painting was finished and doubtless the smiles on the faces passed to tears even before that. The picture is posed, staged, and constructed with a degree of foresight and design. The idea of a moment caught in time is itself a construction. It is suggested by a variety of details including the pent-up energy in the kitten, whose ears are pricked and claws unsheathed. The boy's head is cocked with his eyes cast upward in an expression as wary as the kitten's. He is looking towards someone to see how she or he will react, while the girl looks out, like the kitten, towards us.

As Baxandall has said, the intentions would be modified and developed over time as she built up the painting into a complete and functioning whole. Small details testify to this process of how intentions develop in a way unforeseen at the beginning: for example, there is a three-layered ruff of fur descending down the kitten's chest, which echoes in design and texture the white ruff worn round the girl's neck.

In this painting, as in most successful art, the interdependency of intention, subject matter and process actually depends upon expertise. If Leyster were cack-handed as a painter, if she could not rely upon herself to be able to solve problems as they came up, then the process would have collapsed and the intention remained unrealized.

Ultimately what the artist or studio craftsperson depends on is the achievement of informed spontaneity – sufficient practical knowledge to interpret or find the conceptual or emotional content that is being sought. Informed spontaneity is not to be taken as meaning working very fast, but working knowledgeably and fluently.

For a brief example of intention and process failing to work interdependently, I can offer my experiences in Chapter Three. I recall that when working on my portrait head I could get not get a likeness. The hollow vessel of the head was in constant danger of collapse: I did not want to puncture the walls of the head, nor did I want the structure to fold or sag under its own weight and collapse around the neck. The tendency for the face to become built out beyond the head was a recurrent and unexpected problem. A glimmer of likeness would appear at one part of the head, only to be lost once I moved the head around. The facial structure would come right in places but dissolve into muddle minutes later. I had not intended that.

I will leave the last words on the interdependency of intention and process to Edward Johnston among whose notes on the nature of being a (studio) craftsperson is the following:

a) The craftsman is one who works in substances, making things of them, with special tools and by special methods.
b) He also thinks in substances and in things, and in methods – plans or designs – which direct the tool and form the thing out of the substance.
c) He thinks of substances, things and designs (methods, plans, etc.) as radically inseparable factors in his work.[30]

In this chapter, two themes have been discussed: the first concerned the importance to the individual artist of possessing a genuine subject matter as opposed to a manufactured one; secondly, it has been argued that intention and process are interdependent. Although artists quite naturally have ideas about what and how they will something prior to making it, nonetheless, these intentions are modified (sometimes dramatically) as the process develops. Intention and process are intertwined.

Serious artists and studio craftspeople do not see their 'life's work' realized in one artefact. They continue over years to make works, try out new subjects and explore new areas of practical thinking. What becomes valuable to them as this occurs is a resource of experience and memories – it is these that contribute to the 'artist within'.

6 All Five Senses

Handicraft knowledge is flexible. Oil painting, for example, is perhaps one of the freest forms of generating imagery. The difficulty is in the long process of study that is required to become fluent in the riches it makes possible but it offers a means of being free of the literal world.

Yet some of the anti-handicraft conventions of contemporary art are so ingrained that it takes a considerable effort to question them. One such shibboleth is 'Skill should not be exercized for its own sake.' In other words, the demonstration of skill should not be the purpose and subject matter of a work of art.

Why not? It is acceptable for an artist, such as the contemporary German expressionist Georg Baselitz, to make an excited but blunt gesture as the core of his art; or for Richard Serra, the Minimalist sculptor, to make artisanal metal-working processes the core of his art. But elaborate, fine workmanship is dismissed as 'virtuoso twiddles'.[1] Why never skill for skill's sake? Why is 'risk taking', that axiom of so many late twentieth-century Western artists, only interpreted in terms of flouting conservative taste and seldom as the risk of trying to accomplish an elaborately executed artefact?

It may be true that an object does not often pass muster by virtue of its skill alone; yet it is to be recognized that a lot of medieval and Renaissance work is valued as high art because it is skilled work. In his book *The Renaissance Artist at Work*, Bruce Cole writes, 'Any careful, first-hand examination of Renaissance art reveals that craft is of remarkable importance: paintings and sculpture from the period are among the most beautifully made objects in the entire history of Western art.'[2]

In the twentieth century, the plastic arts, and most particularly the studio crafts, have been regarded, especially by practitioners, as an aesthetic in opposition to the highly polished, accurate production that is supplied by technology.[3] Technology is good at manufacturing neatly made goods and so, goes the argument, we want something that is overtly different: we want to see the artist's hand, spirit, and individuality. Technology brings life's comforts, but we look to the artist to provide human drama – hence the dominance, in one form or another, of 'expressionism'.

Michael Baxandall has argued that handmade art is interesting because we get a sense of the artist's intention changing as his or her work developed. The completed work gives us both a résumé of decisions and the resolution of those decisions.[4] All this tells us little about the man or the woman behind the work but seems to tell us about the process of the work itself – how it evolved and why it is as it is. Industrial design does not do this.

In most industrially designed products the process by which intentions have evolved has been set aside before the manufacturing begins. And although designing may include sketching, drawings, models, and prototypes, it is a process of creative endeavour that is intended to fix all the decisions about the appearance of the object before production begins. The consumer has little or no hint as to how the thing evolved into its current state. There is a distinction between the products of art and the products of design. We value art differently from design because we appreciate the process of the making and the development of the individual work of art. However, although industrial manufacture produces high standards at reasonable prices to the purchaser, the industrialized factory is not a producer of preciousness, its goal is the excellence of tidiness. Occasionally, industry makes bizarre efforts to create exquisite objects and turns its hand to gold-plating cameras or embedding jewels in industrially produced objects in order to attract the undiscerning rich.

Industrial design and manufacture finds it both difficult and uneconomic to generate finesse, especially the finesse of complexity. It is true that there is refinement in the edges and profiles of a plastic moulding or in the curves of a carefully built car, but such refinement is generally bland – blandness is so often the companion of tidiness.

However, few artists have stepped in to supply the exquisite work that industry cannot provide. There are reasons for this absence: a failure to find an appropriate subject matter is one important factor. To produce a work of fine and elaborate workmanship requires a convincing subject. This does not necessarily mean a religious or a moral theme: after all, Italy's most famous goldsmith, Benvenuto Cellini (1500-71), is famous for a salt-cellar which, with its naked male (Neptune) and female (Earth) set amongst sea-horses and dolphins, is a sensuous and sensual tour de force. And although in the West the late twentieth-century is a secular age, and Christianity therefore provides only a few artists with convincing subject matter, the activities of sex, pleasure and happy indulgence (Cellini's subjects) remain topical even if, in a culture fearful of AIDS, it is a matter of wistful and wishful thinking rather than practice.

Contemporary art has not, of course, been wholly antagonistic towards the production of exquisite objects. The (West) German tradition of fine silver and goldsmithing has resulted in a succession of fine small works by artist-craftsmen such as Hermann Jünger, former Professor of Goldsmithing at the Munich Academy of Arts, and in Britain the craftsman-sculptor Michael Rowe[5] has produced a variety of brass vessels, finely constructed in forms that are analogous to modernist architecture: a synthesis of simple rectangular and curved planes, which echo Le Corbusier's chapel at Ronchamp, perhaps. He has used his knowledge of the patination of metals to create some of the most beautiful and subtly coloured and textured surfaces produced in the West since 1945.

Rowe would, of course, reject the suggestion that what he is involved in is 'skill for skill's sake'. As an admirer of his work I would nonetheless dismiss his protestations. The antagonism to the very idea of 'skill for skill's sake' is deep, widespread and almost instinctive among most practitioners, teachers, writers, arts administrators and the rest who make up the arts community. There is at best only the most grudging acceptance of the idea that in the virtuoso display of practical knowledge there are values other than bravado. Skill for skill's sake is regarded as mere trickery, as vacuous an activity as, for instance, writing out the Lord's Prayer on the back of a postage stamp. Yet the display of craft knowledge, the creation of exquisitely executed, elaborate designs can, in itself, be a way of communicating values: care, love, a desire to serve, an intention to delight, a desire to honour a patron, a client or some other, more abstract or metaphysical entity such as 'my country' or 'my God'.

The Wilton Diptych, an English Christian altarpiece from the fourteenth century, combines outstandingly detailed craftsmanship with a devotional purpose.[6] The altarpiece is small and portable, consisting of two hinged panels, painted on all four sides. The artist is unknown, and even the date is uncertain – scholars say the altarpiece was produced between 1395 and 1399. The painting is said to be English but the artist may have been foreign, working at the English court of Richard II, who was King between 1377 and 1399. It shows Richard kneeling, being presented to the Virgin and the Christ-child by the saints John the Baptist, Edward the Confessor and Edmund. The painting is crowded with angels, heraldry, jewels and flowers.

The painting, which is precise in its craftsmanship and emphatic in details such as the gesture of a hand or the turning of a head, puzzles scholars: 'Why is Richard shown with these saints? What does the gesture of his half-open hands mean – are they empty or praying? Why are the figures in the left panel in a wasteland, while the Virgin and Child and angels are in a flowery meadow?'[7]

These questions are important because answers to them would add to our understanding and hence our conceptual pleasure, but what carries the painting across to us is its extraordinary finesse. Or, as the introduction to the 1993 exhibition catalogue says, 'This ... was almost certainly intended for the private religious devotions of Richard II ... and is one of the most beautiful paintings ever made. The intricacy of detail, the refinement and subtlety of its varied techniques and decorative effects, the richness of its colours and the tooling of the gold are unmatched in any surviving painting.'[8]

One does not, I suggest, value the painting for the psychological particularities of the expressions on the faces of the figures. The three saints look equally pious but give no hint of individual thought; the angels, some of whom are making animated gestures, give nothing away, and their faces look very like that of the Virgin herself. For a twentieth-century Western viewer, whose ideological and historical baggage includes Humanism, the Enlightenment and modern psychology, these faces are peculiarly similar. However, amidst the collection of delphic faces, the sharp-nosed, rather prissy looking face of Richard stands out while the relationship between the kneeling King and the Christ-child is almost electric. The altarpiece is brought alive by the reciprocity of the gaze between the child (who is the most animated of the figures and has almost wrested himself from the arms of the Virgin) and Richard.

What would this altarpiece be like to pray to? Very few Christians pray before an image in which they themselves feature in a direct relationship with the subject of their prayer. Assuming that this altarpiece was for Richard II's personal devotions then this diptych might have induced in him a palpable sense of nearness to God. To make sense to a devout king, this relationship had to look physically beautiful: crudity, lack of care, inattention to detail or other slovenliness would be inimical to devotion and distracting to the religious or spiritual reverie that I assume to be one of the 'functions' of this altarpiece.

Who knows what form another person's reverie takes? Yet we know that for a lot of people, one of the characteristics of listening carefully to another person or losing oneself in concentration are similar forms of reverie, that in musing abstractedly the mind wanders over the physical details of whatever happens to be near at hand. The mind plays with details in a conscious yet half-distracted way. Small, highly crafted, elaborately detailed objects such as *The Wilton Diptych* offer both layers of detail and little 'hot spots' of visual information. One studies the modelling of a face, moves on to the delicate patterning of a robe and then lingers, sifting through the detail, of the gold and jewels of a crown. It is to be noted, however, that the exquisiteness of the craftsmanship and the emphatic handling of detail in the diptych is kept in check by a robust but elegant composition.

Craftsmanship can, did, and still does go hand in hand with the conceptual ordering and organization of the work as a whole. There are enough basic clues to indicate the truth of this: look at the layout and design of a craftsperson's workshop, and the design and organization of the processes that he or she employs in each of the tasks of making. In all of these basic aspects there is economy of effort and resources. Economy in anything demands design. Yet there is an insidious assumption, especially prominent in the twentieth century, that to be accomplished in a craft does not include an accomplishment of composition and design. This assumption is the legacy of the division of labour which states: designers think, craftsman do as they are told. It is the old war beween theory, professional status and tacit knowledge (see Chapter One, pp. 10-17). Good craftspeople often demonstrate a 'natural' facility for design because the organization of the parts of an object into a whole flows from the thinking that is involved in the creation and organization of the parts in the first place.

The evidence of the craftsperson as a designer is abundant in examples from the past: in the design of the tools and workshops of the carpenter, mason and blacksmith and also, most strongly, in the home, kitchen and garden.[9] From time to time contemporary designers rediscover 'natural' design and it reappears as the 'English Country Look' or 'Shaker Style' or 'French Agrarian'. In Britain in the late 1940s, when architects and designers were trying to establish a modern vernacular style for streets, squares and other public places, there was a revival of interest in the work that anonymous engineers and artisan-designers had created for the eighteenth-century canal system. In Britain in the 1980s there was a similar revival of interest in the design of one of the greatest craft-based industries: the Victorian railways.

If the quality of design in craft is less obvious today, this is a result of the redistribution and atomization of skills and labour that characterize the professionalization of art, and the marginalization of craft and the splitting of design functions from those of making. Among those who build their own boats, customize their cars and construct their own houses, there is a considerable interest in and talent for designing through making.

Utilitarian design aside, however, the appeal of skill for skill's sake is in the wonder one feels at the audacity of the maker in attempting a work of complexity in which the risk of practical and intellectual failure is present.

In a work such as *The Wilton Diptych* the variety of craft knowledge demonstrated is quite dazzling, while the particular care demanded of each craft technique is apparent even to those of us who are ignorant. Consider, for instance, this passage from the exhibition catalogue:

> One of the distinctive features of the diptych is the variety of ways in which [gold] stippling using a single-dot punch has been used, both for patterning and for modelling, creating subtle effects which exploit the optical qualities of the changing fall of light. The punching was probably done by exerting pressure with a small metal tool, rather than by tapping the punch with a mallet, because of the delicate, light and precise touch needed to indent the gold but not break its surface.[10]

This process is a part of the meaning of the work and our recognition and contemplation of its presence (even if we are unaware of the details of its process) is a part of the primary pleasure to be had in *The Wilton Diptych*; it is not secondary to the 'idea' of the work. It is also a refreshing twist on the contemporary art world orthodoxy of 'risk-taking' in which the only risk taken by the artist is that he or she may offend the spectator. 'Risk-taking' is a popular orthodoxy of contemporary art, especially art education. The phrase has become a familiar weapon in the artist's armoury of self-aggrandisement since it implies artistic courage, iconoclasm and a 'paint and be damned' conviction. But the once noble attitude of risk-taking has become associated with either the rejection of tradition (a stale attitude) or the embrace of novelty (what is there left to try?). The obverse of the contemporary attitude, which encourages risk-taking is hostility towards craft, knowledge and skill, which are seen as 'safe'.

Yet, in the pursuit of a complex craft, artist-craftspeople may genuinely 'risk all' by making errors in the creation of their work, causing them to lose time, effort and money or the work in its entirety. Moreover, where an attempt is made to use a body of craft knowledge and recognized skills then the artist is inviting public and professional scrutiny: other people can see when the artist fails. One of the common risks that complex craft objects entail for their makers is the risk of overworking the material or the subject or both. And it is this deadness that those who distrust handicraft most frequently mention as a reason for rejecting skill. Good skilled artists know these risks: their courage lies in confronting them.

Good craftspeople know as well as anyone else that subjects matter as much as good skills and materials. A Christian artist making a Christian artefact must address the reality that the subject is more important than the artefact he or she is making. The artist is making something for God – and this tends to raise the artist's standards. In the case of *The Wilton Diptych*, the content – Richard II being presented to Christ – must have exerted an extraordinary pressure upon the artist to do his (or her) best, not for himself (or herself), but for the King and for God. The King believed, like many, that he was King by the divine grace of God. Hence the lines in Shakespeare's play *Richard II*: 'The breath of worldly men cannot depose/ The deputy elected by the Lord.'[11]

It is argued that the craft demonstrated by *The Wilton Diptych* is irrelevant to our contemporary needs and beliefs. Indeed, in admiring the diptych one hardly admires the political reality of being governed by authoritarian kings who believe they are doing God's will. Nonetheless, even if the religious sentiment no longer finds favour with us and the political message is repugnant, we still ought not to boast that such art – such craft – as is revealed to us by *The Wilton Diptych* is irrelevant. Arguably the very commitment to fine workmanship is a form of practical idealism. The very doing of such work demonstrates a commitment to quality and to a sense of making something that has intrinsic value; it is idealistic.

This is not to suggest that we should seek literally to copy or revive the subjects, aesthetics and handicrafts of *The Wilton Diptych*: it is to plea for recognition that the greater weight of the aesthetic and emotional content present in an art object is in direct proportion to its skill content.

In modern art and contemporary studio craft the emphasis has been on making overtly expressionist objects. Responding to industrial design's aesthetic of tidiness, the arts and crafts have produced relatively 'crude' texture, form and decoration. Deliberation and planning shapes so much in twentieth-century industrialized culture that there has been widespread desire from people to see, feel and participate in activities that are spontaneous, fluent, quick and free. Fashion, music and dance, for example, have been impelled by a desire for freedom rather than pattern and order.

Freedom in the plastic arts has meant 'mark-making', particularly of a kind that looks as if it has been put down with great energy – energy that is equated by the viewer (correctly or not) with passion. The phrase 'mark-making' is unencumbered by associations of discipline, order and content, and it is as innocent, as untutored in its implications, as is possible.

There is pleasure to be had in both making and seeing a fluent, expressionist gesture, just as there is an almost 'instinctive' response felt by many Westerners for the warmth and variety of randomly or intricately textured objects such as old stone, basket-work and clay brick. Because industry (with some craft-centred exceptions, such as haute couture) is not good at creating products with subtle, interesting or lively surfaces, the plastic artist, be he or she a minimalist working in lead or an 'artist basketmaker', gets a warm reception. We find ourselves thinking that such work is 'alive' and that it is somehow more 'humane' than the products of the aesthetics of tidiness. Mark-making is not only therapy for the artist but for the spectator as well.

There is a craft to creating nuances of texture and, indeed, to sophisticated mark-making which requires discrimination in making and connoisseurship. However, this knowledge of doing and discrimination is easily blunted and lost. If industry now offers blandness, art offers dramatic gesture – but it is frequently crude, lacking nuance and subtlety. When we compare our contemporary efforts at spontaneity with those of the past then we realize how much knowledge has been lost. To some extent this loss has been disguised by frequent changes in artistic fashion and the rapid substitution of one novelty by another.

For example, a feature of twentieth-century industrial culture is to be seen in the way that art, advertising, design, craft and fashion has become super-eclectic. We raid other cultures for ideas. The growth and sophistication of museums, mass travel, photography, film, books, magazines and journals has turned studying the past or studying the cultures of other countries into a form of shopping.

Artists are eclectic. In catalogues to many exhibitions one will read the statements of the artists or the craftspeople in which they explain that they have been, for instance, influenced, excited and inspired by work seen on trips to Mexico or Korea or the Sudan. (Equally, whenever non-Western countries develop industrially, and their artists travel to the West, they in their turn are excited and inspired by their travels. Whenever artists travel, so do ideas about art.)

Twentieth-century studio craftspeople, searching for examples of spontaneity, rawness and freedom in handmade artefacts have understandably been drawn to cultures where handiwork is still central: it may be in Japan or Africa or in neglected working-class communities in the older established industrial cultures.

There is a debt to pay for eclecticism: foreigners may seize upon other people's craft and art but they often get it wrong. They get it wrong in part because what they are looking for is what interests them, and not what was necessarily of interest to the native artist or his or her indigenous audience. As Michael Baxandall makes clear (see p. 79), the notion of influence is not that artist X influences artist Y but that Y finds something of relevance to him in artist X's work. One may view this as cultural appropriation or cultural colonialism, but every instance has to be judged on the particular circumstances. The relationship between Bernard Leach and the potters of Japan, for example, is regarded by the Japanese and the British as mutually beneficial.

Earlier discussions about the difference between regulative and constitutive rules are pertinent here (see Chapter Three, p. 42, and Chapter Four, pp. 60-4). Constitutive rules were described as the rules which constitute our behaviour: they are learned at our mother's breast, our father's knee, our teacher's desk, in our friend's backyard or from our enemies on the street: our culture, in other words. To understand our world any foreigner must 'go native'. When artists borrow from other cultures, they do not 'go native'. What they do with what they take is sometimes inferior, and always different to that produced by the primary culture.

Eclecticism has proved successful in European art where it has led to innovation, such as Matisse's interest in arabesque patterns, but leads to disappointment where the intention has been to imitate the 'alien' culture. This, I believe, is particularly true of pottery. Much that has been produced in studio ceramics has attempted to capture the spontaneity and fluency of Korean, Japanese and Chinese calligraphy in its decoration. Much of it looks successful until one has occasion to see it side by side with the real thing, when one recognizes a loss. By comparison our version looks ill-informed. On the other hand, the influence of Eastern ceramics and calligraphy upon twentieth-century Western studio ceramics has also been beneficial because it provided new ideas about form, shape and texture – ideas which men like Leach were able to use in rekindling interest in indigenous but neglected European ceramic traditions, such as slip-ware and other 'folk' decoration.

The point remains, however, the differences between the work of the culture that has been borrowed from and that of the foreign culture are seldom noticed because, oddly, among the many didatic exhibitions of art, craft and design virtually none of them explore notions of quality in art. There is no curatorial interest in making the criteria about judgments of quality in art transparent. Yet this could be done by contrasting similar but qualitatively different objects.

Certainly, as far as the public's interest in craft is concerned, there is an uncertainty and even ignorance about what to expect from handicraft and this has helped to encourage a presumption that 'handmade' means 'rough, untidy, peasant-like, and homely'. Today's idea is that craft is untidy and that its roughness is proof of its zestful (natural) spontaneity. Consequently, in addition to losing our ability to recognize and produce the exquisite, we have probably lost some of our ability to recognize the aesthetics of informed spontaneity.

I suggested earlier that spontaneity in craftsmanship is not to be confused with quickness. Spontaneity is a quality, it is not necessarily the lightning movement of a conjurer's repertoire. Spontaneity depends on fluency, knowledge and economy. It is a quality we recognize in a drawing or a piece of lettering or the combination of colours which we perceive, with our all our senses, 'to be just so'. We can be misled. Many people claim that the drawings of the letterer and sculptor Eric Gill have this quality, but on closer examination Gill's drawings can often be shown to be meretricious: the lines of his naked women and men often have élan, but they are sometimes in the wrong place. Rodin's drawings are better, as are Lucian Freud's, because they have both élan and accuracy. Equally, the pleasure of Edward Johnston's drawings of letters are satisfying both for the quality of their line and the accuracy of their forms.

The emotional impact of seeing a line set down with accuracy and élan, or a form that looks and feels just right in texture, colour and shape, is impossible to describe but it seems to have its counterpart in every human activity – in the beauty of play by a fluent athlete on the sportsfield, for example, or in the magic of a piece of physics. In each case what is present is beauty.

Artists and art critics currently shy away from the word 'beauty', but physicists embrace it. The physicist and Nobel laureate Steven Weinberg devotes a chapter of his book *Dreams of a Final Theory*[12] to 'beautiful theories'; and he writes, 'there is another quality besides simplicity that can make a physical theory beautiful – it is the sense of inevitability that the theory may give us. In listening to a piece of music or hearing a sonnet one sometimes feels an intense aesthetic pleasure at the sense that nothing in the work could be changed.'[13]

It would going too far to insist that in any or all major sculptures or paintings that the change of a single element would bring ruin to that work: such argument is hyperbole, it is practical nonsense. Nevertheless, the sense of an internal logic, a rightness, and an overwhelming sense that things have come out 'just so' seems to be a common description of many people's appreciation of what makes a work of art pleasurable for them. Simple works of art can quite frequently induce this sensation: there are many pots in the world that are good in just that way.

This sensation of informed spontaneity, fluency or 'rightness' is harder to achieve in more complex works, but when the complex work does achieve this goal then the aesthetic satisfaction it offers is often greater than in minimalist objects.

Outside film and theatre there are relatively few practitioners attempting complex works of handicraft in the plastic arts. One of these is Lucian Freud. In the catalogue accompanying his 1993 London exhibition,[14] the curator, Catherine Lampert, implies that Freud's empirical analyses, craft knowledge, emotional range and virtuosity are nearly exceptional in late twentieth-century art. And although I believe Lampert goes too far in seeming to imply that Freud is the heir to Rembrandt or Velazquez, I agree with her memorable description of Freud's work: 'His is a sensibility that runs all five senses as if wired up together.'[15] The suggestion is that Freud does not try to paint a likeness of flesh but seeks to 'create flesh'. Or rather, that when one sees a figure of Freud's then one 'feels' the weight, as well as the texture, movement or form of the body. This representation, as always with intelligent artists, is an intellectual analogy, an interpretation of reality constructed in and through the craft.

There is relatively little contemporary craft or art of which one can claim that it has the complexity, knowledge and inevitablity of 'all five senses wired together'. Yet in the museums one comes upon such examples from the past.

In the Victoria and Albert Museum, London, there is a collection of maquettes by the Flemish-born Giambologna (1529-1608) who made his career in Florence where he became the most famous sculptor since Michelangelo. Giambologna is described as a mannerist. Mannerism demanded a knowledge and fluency in the rules of craft, including those deduced from classical art and those developed during the Renaissance, but the style itself involved the breaking or straining of these rules. Although the central subject matter in mannerism is the human figure, in the hands of a mannerist sculptor it could be elongated, distorted and forced to emotional and theatrical effect. Mannerist sculpture displays a lot of virtuoso design thinking, and sometimes elaborate or daring compositions become an important part of the sculpture's content.

I have in mind a terracotta maquette by Giambologna that is of a river god: a naked man, semi-recumbent with elongated limbs, an over-long torso twisting to the left, and a roughly modelled leonine head twisted round and gazing into space in a reverie of noble despair.

This model, although it is anatomically wayward, makes a convincing god for this is, appropriately, a fine figure of a man. He has grace, brute power, and intense energy. Giambologna's *River God* is a wonderful example of informed spontaneity and of Lampert's 'all five senses wired together'. It is the product of great talent and of great knowledge – it is a tour de force. A part of its appeal is its aesthetic complexity; it is even a piece of ceramic art in the modern and abstract sense of it being a highly textured, tactile, self-referential 'object'. It has great human interest because it shows a figure of strength, drama and beauty. This particular object has a controlled ambiguity: it has the qualities of a sketch, with the god's face in particular being a ruin: the sculptor's thumb has dragged down from the forehead to the chin. It is because of the ambiguity of the form that the figure appears constantly to move – the ambiguity creates the visual metaphor of the figure being alive. The intensity of Giambologna's *River God* makes the minimalist sculptures of our own age seem insubstantial.

In our age, reductionism and atomization in art has had its effect on what the individual artist can do and, consequently, on the richness of the experience offered to the viewer.

The artists mentioned in this chapter – the anonymous maker(s) of *The Wilton Diptych*, Cellini, Giambologna, and Freud – produced complex, expressive works. The works are not, however, expressive of the individual artist's character or pyschological state. Or, if they are, we have no way of knowing that this is the case. We cannot reliably infer the character or mood of the artist from the art work. But what we can say is that the work is expressive of some (or all) of what each artist knows. This is especially true of the most ostensibly 'expressive' artist of the four listed above, Giambologna. Dr Charles Avery, author of a study on the sculptor, wrote: 'The ingenuity of his solution to a complex problem of design and the technical accomplishment of carving it in marble or casting and chasing it in bronze were paramount in Giambologna's aesthetic.'[16]

Of course it would be foolish to deny the importance of an artist's self-consciousness, psychology and emotional range in the creation of his or her work of art. Indeed, one of the most interesting arguments put by Michael Polanyi in *Personal Knowledge* is the notion that to understand human knowledge we must recognize its sensuous, sensual and emotional context. We do not think, learn, make choices or set intentions for ourselves in the manner of calculating machines, but within contexts where desires, ambitions and competitive aspirations shape our very being. They shape what we know, what we can know, and what we want to know.

Nevertheless, we are not only shaped by our predispositions but also by what we learn to do. Some art is emotionally affective without necessarily having been the product of an overtly self-conscious or philosophical mind. Dr Avery compares Michelangelo and Giambologna in an interesting way: 'Unlike the intense and neurotic genius Michelangelo, Giambologna was not deeply involved with the spiritual content of his work ... Untouched by lofty philosophical concepts beyond his immediate vocation, Giambologna worked fast and methodically.'[17]

Of course, it will be argued Michelangelo is the supreme philosopher-artist and consequently, in terms of Western art, represents the best of all possible worlds. Nonetheless, it may be interesting to reflect on just how many affective works of art draw their power from their maker's practical vocation rather than spiritual aspirations. Moreover, Giambologna's facility with pagan and secular themes translated more than adequately when he began taking major religious commissions. As far as Florence was concerned, Avery describes Giambologna as 'par excellence the sculptor of the Counter-Reformation'.[18] This makes sense because the Roman Catholic reply to the Protestants' theological and doctrinal reformism was to stress the reality of the beliefs and devotional subjects of the Church. If anyone could give a palpable, sensuous reality to Christ, the Virgin Mary and the Saints, it was Giambologna and his studio.

'Know-how' affects the way one sees the world just as surely as emotional temperament or physical and mental health. Even the sorts of exhibitions that we attend can affect our ways of seeing the world and reacting to it: there is, as Ernst Gombrich points out in *Art and Illusion*, much truth in the saying that nature imitates art.[19] To some extent you are what you know. The acquisition of tacit knowledge is an enlargement and extension of one's self. As we have seen, to know a thing tacitly means that one has 'gone native' in that knowledge and that one possesses that knowledge intellectually and physically. To know a craft the individual has to make craft knowledge his or her own so that thinking and doing flow together.

Yet the success of contemporary technological culture is putting a strain on personal, individually owned tacit knowledge. Although industrial technology fails to deliver 'the exquisite', the tactile and the expressive, it makes most manufacturing tasks simpler, by taking the person out of the making.

It may not, however, be good for the artist to have things made simpler. Even photography, which was born a mechanical art, can be made too simple for the good of the serious, ambitious photographer. Since the early 1900s and marketing slogans such as 'You press the button, we do the rest',[20] the mass-produced, foolproof camera has democratized the production of images. True, for years the home photograph was a poor thing: it was over-exposed, under-exposed, fogged, badly composed, had unfortunate shadows or unintended intruding objects. But technology has made up for incompetence and the camera became an early example of a commonplace 'intelligent' machine. Silicon chip engineering does away with the need for humans to judge such matters as exposure times.

Computerized technology is going much further, however, in replacing human craft skills. In the 1980s the home electronic organ was developed to allow the musical ignoramus to play tunes in a variety of instrumental arrangements. In the 1990s the same ignoramus became an instant composer, mixing and matching music from others more expert, past and present. The new machine offers emotional qualities too: upbeat, downbeat, sad, sorrowful, chirpy, cold, imperial, sentimental and so on. And the plastic arts may yet receive their turn, with home painting or sculpture kits using a computer, a robotic arm and software enabling the novice artist to mix and match from the repertoires of anyone from Giotto to Duchamp.

Yet skills possessed by a machine are not the same as skills possessed by a human being. In human beings 'experience' is complex and will involve physical sensation and emotion as well as intellectual apprehension. It may also involve moral or aesthetic value judgments. All of this becomes part of the texture of individually acquired knowledge; and none applies to our description of contemporary 'intelligent' machines.

Sometimes we do not recognize how much we have experienced until we try to remember or relive the experience. Artists may need specific memories if they are engaged in modelling or creating illusionistic representations of some aspect or other of the natural and human world. Powers of observation have to be developed as does memory. The strength of both observation and memory is to some extent related to the task in hand, although some exceptionally observant people, such as the scientist Michael Faraday, had poor memories.[21]

Making art (or science) out of what we see concerns the need to make strategies for getting a closer understanding of what we are trying to make sense of. This essay has taken the view that to understand something well one has to try doing it (and try doing it well). But there are limitations to this approach. In trying to understand a part of the natural or the human world one cannot actually do it. One cannot be another person, a cat, a mountain, a river or whatever one is trying to study, represent or analyse. Instead one watches, draws, models, measures, touches, smells, weighs, examines under a microscope, holds up to the light or kicks the object – in other words one attends to it physically or imaginatively.

Some strategies of attention are superior to others. I think drawing is a more attentive process than photography, but I would not deny that for good photographers the act of taking a photograph is an act of imaginative scrutiny. My preference for drawing as a means of attending is based on the observation that even with a bad drawing one must spend time looking at the subject, whereas most photography is a quick aim-and-shoot affair, unaccompanied, it seems, by proper observation.

Peter Gullers, a photographer, explains that good photographers want to internalize the sort of knowledge (especially the tacit knowledge) that goes with the craft of scrutiny – they do not want to leave decisions to their 'intelligent' cameras. Decisions made by clever cameras are dumb: cameras do not have a choice – they are not allowed by their programs to take intentionally wrong decisions. Indeed, intentionality does not (yet) come into the sales descriptions of machines. A 'clever' camera selects on the basis of statistical information. Decisions made by the photographer are genuine decisions – the photographer has a choice, he or she can make a judgment, and he or she can deliberately take the 'wrong' choice.

Gullers's thoughts on the use of automated light-meters and the effect of delegating skill and knowledge to the intelligent machine are quoted at length in a paper called 'The Practice of the Use of Computers'.[22] Gullers says that new technology has made it easier to take photographs reliably and accurately in normal conditions. When there is not enough light, the exposure is blocked or a built-in flash is activated to ensure satisfactory results.[23] However, the program cannot be modified and the underlying principles (which are in effect a hidden expert system) are invisible.

Gullers photographs landscape and industrial scenes and he describes the work like this: 'If I am in a smithy or in a rolling mill shop, I note how the light coming through the sloping skylights contrasts with the sooty heat of the air in the brick building. The vibrations from the hammers and mills make the floor and camera tremble, which makes photography more difficult ... In a new situation, I recall similar situations and environments that I have encountered earlier. They act as comparisons and my previous perceptions, mistakes and experiences provide the basis for my judgment.'[24]

An aspect of creativity revealed by Gullers is the interplay between what we see now and how we have interpreted what we have seen in the past. He blames the technology in his camera for denying him access to his memories and blunting his perceptions. One can say that computers of all kinds, including those in automatic cameras, are a means of making available the effects of other people's skills to an individual without that individual having to acquire them. However, by acquiring no skills for oneself, then one is liable to be trapped by other people's thinking. The unskilled individual cannot override the principles in the machine.

Gullers is right that our perceptions are enriched by involving ourselves actively with the world via a practical and exploratory medium. Here is where a concept of self-fulfilment through handicraft is relevant. For although this essay holds a tacit warning against taking the concept of individuality in the plastic arts too literally – on the grounds that it leads to intellectual, aesthetic and practical autism – nevertheless, one of the rewards of being an artist is the freedom to engage with the world on one's own terms. It is one of the reasons for being a painter, potter, sculptor or calligrapher.

What is especially valuable about craft is that once it is possessed by the individual it cannot be taken away and becomes a massive addition to the individual's life. To know how is a much more powerful and enriching position to be in than merely to know of something. Ultimately, the continuance of handicraft technologies depends upon whether or not people wish to continue to be passive participants in the world of experience by being in the hands of other or whether they are to have experiences and memories of their own. After all, as Wittgenstein put it, 'the world is my world'.[25]

This is a point of fundamental interest. Even if we develop a technology that outwits us as individuals at every turn in thought, word and deed, it would only underline two commonplace features of human culture.

First, whatever one's discipline there is, for most of us, someone better than oneself. Secondly, nonetheless, the world remains your world just as it remains mine. Consequently what someone else knows may be of interest to us individually but of ultimate importance to us is that which we ourselves know. When we possess and make knowledge our own then it enriches our individual worlds.

It is of no qualitative difference to me if Giambologna turned out to be a machine rather than a human being. I would still dearly like to be able to model as well as Giambologna. This wish will not be fulfilled but what remains possible is to have some understanding and some of the pleasures of Giambologna by attempting to create things by hand in clay for myself, even though I know my efforts may be inept. The struggle provides intellectual and practical pleasure, interest and possibly insight. And indeed, it is on the basis of just such reasoning that the whole plethora of amateur activity is grounded and valued.

The serious amateur, however, is no dilly-dallying Peter Londoner. The amateur craves real knowledge in his or her chosen activity and will be as eager and as competitive as the best professional, because it is the striving for expertise that is open to public scrutiny and competitive testing that makes the knowledge worth incorporating into ourselves.

The good professional is in a similar position to that of the amateur because he or she must acknowledge there are women and men better than themselves. But it is no help to the individual to give up being a professional artist. To deny oneself the freedom to do what one wants to do simply because others are better is to commit a form of suicide. The converse is also true: to refuse to acknowledge that others are better than oneself is to retreat into autism, which in itself is professional suicide, because it amounts to a refusal to learn from others.

The process of acquiring craft knowledge is not easily or naturally done by an individual in isolation. Although tacit knowledge is 'my knowledge', it is also communal. For, in whatever craft discipline one chooses, there is a body of knowledge which shapes our perceptions about our work and our individual worlds.

The flexibility and variety of craft knowledge that has been built up in the plastic arts is in itself a rich technology. In this technology there are ideas for the future. But craft knowledge is wearing thin, it is being lost. In my view, the loss of handicraft technology would be as great a cultural loss as the disappearance of the great cathedrals. If the loss continues, it will be not only as a consequence of computerization, but of our response to it. Currently our response in the plastic arts is to adopt a self-defeating individuality of self-expression. It will be lost through the failure to recognize that 'We are unique, I am commonplace'.

Notes on the Text

Introduction

1 Thompson, J., *Gravity and Grace* exhibition catalogue, The South Bank Centre, London 1993, pp. 17-21.

2 Frayling, C. and Snowden, H., *Perspectives in Craft*, published in *Crafts Classics*, Crafts Council, London 1988, pp. 120-1.

3 Greenberg, C., from *After Abstract Expressionism*, in *Art International VI*, No. 8, 1962, pp. 24-32. Republished in *Art in Theory 1900-1990* edited by Harrison, C. and Wood, P., Blackwell, Oxford 1992, pp. 767-9.

4 *Ibid.*

Chapter One: What Is Craft Knowledge?

1 Schwartz, J., *The Creative Moment*, Cape, London 1992.

2 *Ibid.*

3 Rosenbrock, H. H., 'Engineering as an Art', in *Artificial Intelligence, Culture and Language: On Education and Work*, edited by Goranzon, B. and Flavin, M., Springer-Verlag, Berlin and Heidelberg 1990, pp. 95-7.

4 Polanyi, M., *Personal Knowledge*, Routledge, London 1983, p. 52.

5 This refers to the European Side Impact Dummy research project conducted by Ogle Design, UK and TNN of the Netherlands and others between 1983 and 1993.

6 Collins, H., *Changing Order*, Sage, London 1985, pp. 53-78.

7 *Ibid.*

8 Janik, A., 'Tacit Knowledge, Working Life and Scientific Method', in *Knowledge, Skill and Artificial Intelligence*, edited by Goranzon, B. and Josefson, I., Springer-Verlag, Berlin and Heidelberg 1988, pp. 62-3.

9 The conference was held in Stockholm, Sweden, in May and June 1988. The papers have been published under the title *Artificial Intelligence, Culture and Language: On Education and Work, op. cit.*

10 See note 8: Janik explains that 'it requires considerable diligence to be in a position to be able to articulate a situation in working life – and this is crucial – to the point where we can grasp why it eludes precise description.'

11 Pye, D., *The Nature and Art of Workmanship*, Cambridge University Press 1968, pp. 24-9.

12 Wallis, B., 'Artist or Engineer?', published in *Royal Designers on Design*, The Design Council, London 1986, pp. 86-95.

13 Hare, D., *Murmuring Judges*, Faber & Faber, London 1991.

14 Josefson, I., 'Language and Experience', in *Artificial Intelligence, Culture and Language, op. cit.*, pp. 73-4.

15 Polanyi, M., *Personal Knowledge, op. cit.*, pp. 50-1.

16 *Ibid.*

17 Shute, N., *Trustee from the Toolroom*, Heinemann, London 1960, pp. 64-5.

18 Gordon, J., *A Stepladder to Painting*, Faber & Faber, London 1962, p. 65.

19 Polanyi, M., *Personal Knowledge, op. cit.*, p. 49.

20 Janik, A., 'Tacit Knowledge, Working Life and Scientific Method', *op. cit.*, p. 54.

21 Heron, P., 'Late Matisse' in *Modern Painters*, Vol. 6, No. 1, London 1993, pp. 10-19.

22 Janik, A., 'Tacit Knowledge, Rule-Following and Learning', in *Artificial Intelligence, Culture and Language, op. cit.*, p. 49.

23 *Ibid.*

24 It is the creativity inherent in the drill that some crafts entail that enables the practitioner to become interested in solving problems and being creative. This is, as I understand it, a major part of Janik's thesis.

Chapter Two: Craft Skill and the Plastic Arts

1 Britton, A., 'The manipulation of skill on the outer limits of function', *Beyond the Dovetail* exhibition catalogue, Crafts Council, London 1991.

2 Krauss, R., 'A View Of Modernism', *Artforum*, New York 1972, pp. 48-51; republished in *Art in Theory, op. cit.*

3 Walker, J. A., 'Display not to indicate Conceptual Art', letter published in *Art Monthly*, London, May 1993. Walker cites Burgin's *Bracketed Performance*, 1971.

4 *Ibid.*

5 Latour, B., 'Are we talking about skills or about the redistribution of skills?', in the collected papers of 'Rediscovering Skill' conference, Bath Science Studies Centre, University of Bath, UK, September 1990, pp. 96-101.

6 Moszynska, A., *Abstract Art*, Thames and Hudson, London 1990, p. 229.

7 Sweet, D., *Towards a Militant Academy*, Faculty of Fine Art, Metropolitan University of Manchester, 1993.

8 Heron, P., 'Late Matisse', *op. cit.*

9 Cooper, E., *On The Edge: Art Meets Craft* exhibition catalogue, Aberystwyth Arts Centre, Wales 1993, p. 44.

10 Harrison is the author of an important work on practical thinking, *Making and Thinking: a study of intelligent activities*, Harvester Press, London 1978.

11 Britton, A., *op. cit.*

12 *Ibid.*

13 *Ibid.*

14 *Ibid.*

15 Ruskin, J., *The Elements of Drawing*, George Allen, London 1907, p. 3.

16 Gordon, J., *A Stepladder to Painting, op. cit.*, pp. 63-79.

17 Freud, L., *Works on Paper* exhibition catalogue, South Bank Board, London 1988, p. 23.

Chapter 3: Learning a Craft

1 Weil, S., *Seventy Letters*, Letter No. 10, Oxford 1965, pp. 20-3.

2 *The Cutting Edge* exhibition, curated by Janet Barnes, The Ruskin Gallery, Sheffield, UK, 1992.

3 Gullers S., 'Automation-Skill-Apprenticeship', in *Knowledge, Skill and Artificial Intelligence, op. cit.*, p. 35.

4 Johnston, E., *Formal Penmanship*, edited by Child, H., Lund Humphries, London 1971.

5 Janik, A., 'Tacit Knowledge, Rule-Following and Learning', *op. cit.*, p. 50.

6 Collins, H., *Changing Order, op. cit.*

7 Widdershoven, G. A. M., 'A Narrative Theory of Skill', in the collected papers of 'Rediscovering Skill' conference, *op. cit.*

8 Tracy, W., *Letters of Credit*, Gordon Fraser, London 1986, pp. 30-32.

9 Camp, A., *Pen Lettering*, A. & C. Black, London 1984.

10 *Ibid.*

Chapter Four: Do Experts Follow Rules?

1 Rees, R., *Simone Weil: a sketch for a portrait*, Oxford University Press, London 1966, pp. 10-11.

2 Hardy, G. H., *A Mathematician's Apology*, Canto, Cambridge University Press, 1992, pp. 67-8.

3 *Ibid.*, p. 33 (C. P. Snow's introduction to Hardy's text).

4 West, T. G., *In the Mind's Eye*, Prometheus Books, New York, 1991.

5 *Ibid.*

6 *Ibid.*, p. 11.

7 Janik, A., 'Tacit Knowledge, Working Life and Scientific Method', *op. cit.*, pp. 51-63.

8 See in particular Johannessen, K. S., 'Rule-Following and Intransitive Understanding', published in *Artificial Intelligence, Culture and Language, op. cit.* It is only right to point out that the individual reader finds a great flexibility in applying a structure to Wittgenstein to get the interpretation that most suits the reader's taste. Because of the aphoristic, poetic structure of Wittgenstein's writing the reader can all too easily legitimize the meaning he or she wants to find. However, I think the interpretation offered in this essay regarding Wittgenstein on rules is fairly standard.

9 Wittgenstein, L., *Philosophical Investigations*, Blackwell, Oxford 1968.

10 Johannessen, K. S.; see note 8 above.

11 Dreyfus, H. L., 'Is Socrates to Blame for Cognitivism?', published in *Artificial Intelligence, Culture and Language, op. cit.*

12 *Ibid.*, p. 222.

13 *Ibid.*, p. 224.
14 *Ibid.*, p. 227.
15 *Ibid.*
16 Milner, M., *On Not Being Able to Paint*, Heinemann, London 1981.
17 *Ibid.*, p. 3.
18 *Ibid.*, p. 4.
19 *Ibid.*, p. 74.
20 *Ibid.*
21 *Ibid.*, p. 65.
22 *Ibid.*, pp. 17-18.
23 Gordon, J., *A Stepladder to Painting, op. cit.*, p. 76.

Chapter Five: Form and Content

1 Wilenski, R. H., *The Modern Movement in Art*, Faber & Faber, London 1927.
2 *Ibid.*, p. 23.
3 Greenberg, C., 'Modernist Painting', reprinted in *Art in Theory, op. cit.*, p. 756.
4 Moszynska, A., *Abstract Art, op. cit.*, p. 226-8.
5 Gray, N., *Lettering as Drawing*, Oxford University Press, London 1971.
6 *Ibid.*, p. 169.
7 *Ibid.*
8 *Ibid.*, pp. 1-4.
9 Schier, F., 'Painting after Art', reprinted in *Art in Theory, op. cit.*, p. 1112.
10 London, P., *No More Secondhand Art: Awakening the Artist Within*, Shambahla, Boston 1989.
11 See also Cole, B., *The Renaissance Artist at Work*, John Murray, London 1983, p. 33.
12 London, P., *No More Secondhand Art, op. cit.*, p. 45.
13 *Ibid.*, pp. 45-6.
14 Berlin, S., *Alfred Wallis: Primitive*, Redcliffe, Bristol 1992.
15 *Ibid.*, p. 83.
16 Farr, D., *English Art 1870-1940*, Oxford University Press, 1978, p. 247
17 Berlin, S., *Alfred Wallis, op. cit.*, p. 83.
18 *Ibid.*, p. 67.
19 *Ibid.*
20 Baxandall, M., *Patterns of Intention*, Yale, 1986.
21 *Ibid.*, p. 69.
22 *Ibid.*, p. 63.
23 Johnston, E., *Formal Penmanship, op. cit.*, p. 142.
24 *Ibid.*, p. 142.
25 *Ibid.*
26 *Ibid.*
27 Baxandall, M., *Patterns of Intention, op. cit.*, p. 62.
28 *Ibid.*, p. 59.
29 Schama, S., *The Embarrassment of Riches*, Collins, London 1987, p. 553.
30 Johnston, E., *Formal Penmanship, op. cit.*, p. 141.

Chapter Six: All Five Senses

1 Alison Britton referred to 'virtuoso twiddles' in her essay 'The

manipulation of skill on the outer limits of function' (see Chapter Two, p. 33). To be fair to her argument, if one looks at post-modern design, especially in the applied arts, there is much fiddling around with horribly designed details for no apparent reason. But in truth the inability of many artists (including architects) to create successful, detailed and well-wrought decoration is just one of a number of indications that the applied arts in the last quarter of the twentieth century were in a state of confusion rather than the pluralistic health so fondly described by some contemporary critics. Contemporary failure should not be used as an attack upon the tradition of skill, virtuosity and elaboration.

2 Cole, B., *The Renaissance Artist at Work, op. cit.*, pp. 32-3.

3 I have put this argument myself in a chapter headed 'An Aesthetic in Opposition', *The Meanings of Modern Design*, Thames and Hudson, London 1990.

4 Baxandall, M., *Patterns of Intention, op. cit.*, in his chapter 'Intentional Visual Interest'.

5 Rowe, M. and Hughes, R., *The Colouring, Bronzing and Patination of Metals*, Crafts Council, London 1982, republished by Thames and Hudson, London 1991.

6 *The Wilton Diptych* exhibition catalogue, National Gallery Publications, London 1993.

7 *Ibid.*, p. 11.

8 *Ibid.*, pp. 11-12.

9 Simon Schama's book *The Embarrassment of Riches, op. cit.* contains a powerful description of the way in which 'making and doing' was also a part of the design, the ritual and the ideology of domestic life in Holland in the seventeenth century, a tradition which to some extent still appears to guide design in Dutch life.

10 *The Wilton Diptych* exhibition catalogue, *op. cit.*, p. 78.

11 William Shakespeare, *Richard II,* Act III, scene ii, lines 56-7.

12 Weinberg, S., *Dreams of a Final Theory,* Hutchinson Radius, London 1993.

13 *Ibid.*, p. 107.

14 Lampert, C., *Lucian Freud* exhibition catalogue, Whitechapel Art Gallery, London 1993.

15 *Ibid.*, p. 13.

16 Avery, C., *Giambologna*, Phaidon, London 1987.

17 *Ibid.*, p. 9.

18 *Ibid.*, p. 202.

19 Gombrich, E. H., *Art and Illusion,* Phaidon, London 1968, p. 203.

20 This advertising slogan of Kodak was probably coined around 1888 by George Eastman, the pioneer of roll film and snapshot photography.

21 West, T. G., *In the Mind's Eye, op. cit.*

22 Goranzon, B., 'The Practice of the Use

of Computers', published in *Knowledge, Skill and Artificial Intelligence, op. cit.*, pp. 13-14.

23 *Ibid.*

24 *Ibid.*

25 Wittgenstein, L., *Tractatus Logico-Philosophicus,* entry 5.641, Routledge and Kegan Paul, London 1961.